Journey To A Far Place

VISUAL STUDIES

a series edited by Douglas Harper

· J O U R N E Y ·

To A Far Place

AUTOBIOGRAPHICAL REFLECTIONS

Richard Quinney

TEMPLE UNIVERSITY PRESS

Philadelphia

Temple University Press, Philadelphia 19122
Copyright © 1991 by Temple University. All rights reserved
Published 1991
Printed in the United States of America

The paper used in this publication meets the minimum
requirements of American National Standard for Information
Sciences—Permanence of Paper for Printed Library Materials,
ANSI Z39.48-1984 ∞

Library of Congress Cataloging-in-Publication Data
Quinney, Richard.
    Journey to a far place : autobiographical reflections / Richard Quinney.
      p.   cm. — (Visual studies)
    Includes bibliographical references.
    ISBN 0-87722-725-X (alk. paper)
    1. Quinney, Richard.   2. Criminologists—United States—Biography.
    3. Sociologists—United States—Biography.   I. Title.   II. Series.
    HV6023.Q56A3   1990
    364′.092—dc20
    [B]   89-20651
                                                    CIP

CONTENTS

PREFACE

To CONSIDER ONE'S LIFE in autobiographical reflection is in the same tradition as the religious journey. As with the pilgrim, the modern traveler places a life in the context of something greater than itself. One's life derives meaning for itself by the relation of that life to the human community and to the nature of the whole world. And in the course of autobiographical reflection, one begins to seek a higher calling in the life that remains. In an awareness of the divine, the transcendent, the spiritual traveler attends to the needs of human existence.

The "hero on the journey" is one of the oldest and most pervasive myths. Leaving the threshold of home, the hero journeys through an unfamiliar world filled with strangely intimate forces, some threatening and others giving aid and sustenance, and reaches a triumphant end represented by the gaining of insight and wisdom and a union with the creator. The traveler is able then to return home.

Life lived as a journey is a life lived deliberately. With an awareness of the human need to concentrate on life's journey, Henry David Thoreau built a cabin and lived for two years in the woods in the solitude of nature to contemplate and intensify the meaning of life. In *Walden* he wrote: "I went to the woods because I wished to live deliberately, to front only the essential facts of life, and see if I could not learn what it had to teach, and not, when I came to die, discover that I had not lived." In the experience of everyday life—in the woods of everyday life—I too am contemplating and living life deliberately as a journey.

Through autobiographical reflection, then, we come finally to the pilgrimage. Driven by the desire for satisfactions that are not supplied in an existence devoid of the transcendent, we seek now to live deliberately in relation to a larger meaning in the universe. As the monk in moments of silence realizes, life becomes a journey into the unknown. Although the infinite realms of mystery remain, characterizing the essence of the world, we seek a form that permits us once again to practice a meaning in the world. We find our true home in the search for a place in the world. We arrive home when we realize our oneness with all the mystery of the world.

I use the essay to tell the story of my search for home. These essays are autobiographical, a record of, and a reflection on, my journey into the unknown. Through a recounting of the concrete experiences of my everyday life and through a reflection on these events, I hope to gain an understanding of who I am, what I was, and what I may become. Telling the story in the meditative essay, I attend to my common place in the universe.

The writing of these essays is part of the process of living my life deliberately as a journey. It is an attempt to hear and to speak and to act in a way that will bring a life to the far place that is home. Our daily lives and our daily reflections are of ultimate consequence. The meaning of life is in the mindful attention that we give to the mystery of our everyday lives—on a journey to a far place.

Journey To A Far Place

· *A Place Called Home* ·

A LONG TIME AGO, before heaven and earth, there was the greatest mystery of all. The mystery had no place to dwell; it was without a home. Then, from the energy of the sorrow of its longing, the mystery created a place to live. Out of the darkness came light.

It took unnumbered years before all the energy in the longing could come together to make the land. Elements and particles took shape, and in a rush of mighty winds that swept the sky, stars and planets began to take form. Gas and dust and rocks crashed together to make spheres. One sphere, to be called Earth, took its place in orbit around a sun in the far corner of a brilliant galaxy. On a spiraling arm of the Milky Way, human beings found their time and place in the universe.

But before they could appear, the crust of the earth and the atmosphere that encircled the earth had to form, and change, and become something new. From deep in the planet, fire issued forth and made mountains. Volcanoes and earthquakes filled the days and nights with sound and movement and fire. As lightning flashed over the rich waters, microscopic organisms began to appear. Blades of green sprang from the moist soil around the shores. Insects and tiny water creatures began to swim. Life eventually teemed along the tidal flats and marshes, and animals

with feathers and wings took to the air. More complex animals came into being. In time came the animal that walked upright on two hind legs.

On a northern portion of the earth, tilted away from the sun, wondrous things were happening. The beds of great oceans were becoming land. In the valleys, new bodies of water were forming. The land's surface continued to shift and to reshape itself. Sheets of ice slowly moved southward, cutting and dredging. A final glacier edged its way to the southern borders of the place that would come to be known as Wisconsin. As this last glacier receded, the land was left in the form that exists today: Deposits of rock and sand and soil make the rolling hills of southern Wisconsin. Moraines rise along the far horizon. Kettles brimming with water nestle in the woods of farmland. Rivers and creeks wind through the fertile prairie.

A part of this land in southern Wisconsin lay in Walworth County. In this county was the township of Sugar Creek, and within this township was a farm, five miles north of the little town of Delavan. A shallow valley left by the glacier ran through the middle of the farm. Muskrats built their houses on the fringes of ponds that lay at the foot of gently sloping hills. Red-winged blackbirds returned each spring to the marshes, and cowslips sprang up among the bogs. Red-tailed hawks soared all summer long above the giant oak trees. In winter, snow covered the ground, and all was still except for an occasional field mouse making its way from one hole to another.

There were people on this land long before the white settlers came. The earliest inhabitants—"Indians" they were to be called—lived in a sacred union with earth, air, and water. To them, human life was an integral part of the natural world. To them, the land was host to all that is. Birth was a coming out of the land; death was a fulfillment of the promises of the universe. Nature itself was the great mystery, the source of everything.

The settlers that came to Walworth County displaced the tribes that once had been on the land: the Chippewa, the Ottawa, and the Potawatomi. The Indians were forced from their native land, and most of those who survived moved to areas west of the Mississippi. The farm with its marshes, ponds, and woodlands was settled in the 1860s by immigrants from Ireland. Their name was Quinney. On the homestead a new generation was born. The son who stayed on the land had children, and one of his sons farmed the place after him. That farmer in turn had two sons who grew up on the farm. Eventually the sons left home, the elder leaving Wisconsin to teach and to lecture and to wander much of his adult life from one place to another.

One day the son who left Wisconsin began to wonder about the old place he had left thirty years before. Like many others before him, he found himself asking questions about his own beginnings. His life was half over; now it seemed to be turning back on itself. The road he was taking was toward a place called home.

•

On a summer day in 1980, as he drove toward the airport in a gentle rain, the hazy gray sky-line of Providence, Rhode Island, receded in the rear-view mirror. His wife and his younger daughter were with him. They would drive back to their house in the city as soon as he removed his suitcase from the back of the car. As he left the interstate highway and drove through the entrance of the airport, he wondered again about the wisdom of making this trip back to the farm.

It had been ten years since he had made the trip to the farm to attend his father's funeral. He had received word one evening in early winter that his father had died that afternoon while walking from the tractor to the tool shed. He had taken the first flight from New York. A cousin had met him at the Milwaukee airport, and they had driven in a snowstorm the sixty miles west to the farm. He remembered his mother standing in a daze, halfway between the house and the barn, as they entered the driveway. Since that time, he had missed his father. Tears still came to his eyes when he thought of him.

His mother had continued to live on the farm after his father's death. From her kitchen window she could look down the road and over the hill to the county highway. The houses of widowed farm women dotted the horizon. His mother's land now was rented out to another farmer's son, who had expanded his acreage to keep his farm going. She had made new friends after her husband's death, had volunteered to work in a rest home in town, and had adjusted in a way to being a farmer's widow whose sons had left the farm. Occasionally, the younger son, a banker in northern Wisconsin, would drive down to the farm to check on her and to help with the few remaining chores. She dreaded the day when she would be too old to live out in the country. Who would care for her? Where would she live? Why had her children never been encouraged to stay on the farm?

The years since the older son had left the farm had been filled with travel. After his college years, and after he had married and begun his own family, he flew to one place or another as part of his expanding professional life. There were the lectures he was asked to present in his chosen field. Each year he attended professional meetings either to present papers on contemporary social problems or to chair sessions that he had organized for the meetings. He had flown numerous times for job interviews in universities located in towns and cities throughout the country. There were sabbaticals and occasional trips to Europe. And all his travels seemed to take him farther away from the farm in Wisconsin.

The jet engines roared and the plane raced down the runway, climbing steeply as it swung out over the bay. Turning westward, it rose above the clouds and headed for Chicago. The stewardess placed a tray of soft scrambled eggs, melted cheese, and sausages in front of him. He picked at his food, trying to avoid too large a dose of cholesterol. While growing up on the farm, he had consumed enough animal fat to last a lifetime.

In many ways his adult life could be regarded as successful. He had been fortunate in his marriage. His children had given him great joy. His career as a university professor and research scholar had on most counts been rewarding. His ideas and theories, propounded in articles and books, were judged by his colleagues to be original and stimulating. His recently published book, *Providence*, was a philosophical treatise on the need to bring spiritual concerns into intellectual inquiry for the purpose of reconstructing the social and moral order. There had never been any question of the seriousness of his pursuits or the moral commitment of his writings and actions. Yet, from his own perspective, something seemed to be missing, both in his work and in his life. Questions were arising that did not fit into the confines of a conventional academic career: Where did we come from? Why are we here? Where is one's home in this world? More and more, his questions were taking him back to his boyhood.

The plane's silver wings with their powerful engines continued to cut through the morning clouds. The checkerboard of midwestern fields was plainly visible at thirty thousand feet. Soon the eastern shores of Lake Michigan would come into view, and the plane would begin its descent. Below, he could see some of the tallest buildings in the world. The plane lowered over the Chicago suburbs. The landing gear came down. The wheels touched and raced along the runway of O'Hare International Airport. The farm was ninety miles to the north.

He was in time to catch the morning bus that would take him to Delavan. Men and women attired for the day's work hurried to meet their flights. Others waited for paneled buses to take them in one direction or another from the airport. He went directly to the rotunda where the small blue bus was waiting. Jet and auto fumes filled the air around the buses. He caught his breath—partly from excitement—as he took his seat.

The bus made its way into traffic and was soon on Interstate 90. Next it would turn off the interstate and take one of the smaller highways through the farm country of northern Illinois and southern Wisconsin. The territory was familiar to him. He had traveled these roads many times while he was growing up. On winter nights he and Terry and Lee had driven to high school basketball games to write stories for the school newspaper. He had gone with girlfriends to Chicago to attend musicals and movies in majestic theaters along State Street. Once he and his brother had driven to Chicago to see the wonders of Maxwell Street. With his father and several farm neighbors, he used to go to see the Cubs play baseball at Wrigley Field. He had driven these roads back and forth from Evanston on cold winter days while attending Northwestern University, the same roads that his father's aunt and sister had traveled every weekend for years while they were working as seamstresses and maids in the houses of the rich in a fashionable section of Chicago.

He decided to walk the five miles from Delavan. Nearly a hundred years earlier, his great-grandmother Bridget had walked the distance both ways every Sunday to attend Mass at the Catholic church in town. He and his brother would sometimes ride their bicycles to high school and back. And on warm spring days they would sometimes walk to school. The walk from town gave him more time to think.

He turned off the blacktop of County Trunk O onto the gravel road that led to the farm. The sun was setting in the late summer sky. Several small houses had been constructed on subdivided tracts cut out from a neighbor's field. All that remained of the old Dutcher place was the pump at the well and a dilapidated sheep shed; the post-and-beam barn had been pulled down the year before. The place of the original homestead was at the bottom of the hill. The lilac bushes marked the location of the foundation of the old house. Now the family farm was in view.

In name, he was not the same person returning to his home. He had gone away from the place with one name; he was coming back with another. He had been given an old-fashioned name, one that did not lend itself to a nickname. Early in his professional career—after leaving the farm, after attending college and graduate school—he had changed his name to something that sounded less like the sound of the country. But whenever he returned to Delavan and the farm, he was called by the name that his parents had given him.

He walked into the driveway and headed straight to the door of the back porch. The Chinese elms, planted by his father and mother all around the yard in the early years of their marriage, enclosed the lawn and the house. Hesitantly, he knocked at the back door and waited. After what seemed a long time, he heard footsteps behind the door. His mother cracked open the door. "Earl," she said, peering out, "what brings you here?"

•

The earliest memory in Earl's life was of his father's father coming across the field from the homestead to help with the morning chores. It was to be the last year of John Quinney's life. He would die in 1939 when Earl was five years old. Earl's dad said, "Here comes the old man."

Neighbors talked in hushed tones when either Earl or his younger brother, Ralph, would ask about their grandfather Quinney. Few details remain of the old man's seventy-nine years of life in Sugar Creek Township. As well as a farmer, he had been a trader of work horses. He bought them when they were young and trained them to be suitable for working the fields. He was a large and strong man, and people said he could "break a horse with one arm." Ma once told the boys that he had been kind to his grandchildren.

John Quinney had married Hattie Reynolds of nearby Rock County shortly before the turn of the century. Hattie died a few years later of consumption, leaving John with two daughters, Marjorie and Nellie, and a son, Floyd. A year after her mother's death, little Nellie died at the age of eighteen months after choking on a raw green pea. John Quinney never remarried. Floyd would tell his own sons what the old man had always told him: "I could never find another woman who would be as good to my children as Hattie was."

Ireland's potato famine of the 1840s had brought John's parents to this country from County Kilkenny. John Quinney's father, whose name was also John, sailed from Ireland to New York in 1849, three years after Bridget O'Keefe had immigrated to the United States from the same townland in County Kilkenny. Both John and Bridget settled in Yonkers, married, and there Bridget gave birth to two of their five children. Not long afterward, the lure of farmland and a new life in Wisconsin must have inspired them to move by steamboat up the Hudson, through the Erie Canal, across the Great Lakes to Milwaukee, and finally to the village of Millard in Walworth County, sixty miles west of Lake Michigan. There they rented a farm until they earned enough by 1868 to purchase the thirty acres for the homestead. The site is still called "the old place."

Bridget lived forty years past the death of her husband, John. She is pictured in a family album, sitting among the lilac bushes in front of the white frame house, smoking her Irish clay pipe. Earl's father would tell his sons stories about how she and the other Irish farm women would gather on Monday mornings to wash and rinse the week's clothes along the sandbar that jutted out from the muskrat pond across the field.

John and Bridget's daughter Kate, who worked as a dressmaker and seamstress, lived all her life at the old place. Their son Tom left the homestead for South Dakota when he was young and settled on a small farm eight miles south of Alexandria. Their son Bill also made his way to South Dakota, where he secured a homestead after the government opened the land for settlement west of the Missouri. When Bill died, his obituary notice, mailed back to Wisconsin, stated that he was "possessed of a friendly disposition" and that he was "well liked by all who knew him." Earl's father always gave the impression that Bill was not a hard worker and that his nature was perhaps too easygoing.

John and Bridget's youngest child, daughter Mary, lived her entire life within fifteen miles of her birthplace. She married Henry Reynolds, and they farmed on the edge of Lake Como. A photograph shows them with farm neighbors and relatives gathered beneath a huge oak tree for the wedding of their daughter. Mary and Henry's son Howard, at the auctioning of the Reynolds

farm in the 1940s, an event that marked an end to Howard's lifetime of farming, gave Earl a bay riding horse named Lady. The prettiest horse ever found on a farm in Earl's opinion, Lady had been trained to neckrein and to run that smoothest of gaits, the single-foot.

Yellowing photographs also show Earl's aunt Marjorie standing in long dresses in the yard at the old place. For most of her short life, Marjorie worked with her aunt Kate, tending the homes of the rich in Chicago. In the summertime, Marjorie worked in the houses and cottages of the same wealthy families who vacationed around Delavan Lake. Only years later, after Marjorie's death at age forty, did Earl's father reveal that she had owned and operated a tavern a few miles southwest of Delavan during the last years of her life. Wherever Earl lived after he left the farm, he kept a framed picture of Marjorie on top of his bookcase.

While Earl was growing up, his father's age was easy to remember. Being born at the dawn of the twentieth century—in the year 1900—his father was always the age of the new year. His birthday came in March as the Wisconsin winter was beginning to show signs of breaking. He farmed all his life on the old place, adding a few acres each year to increase the size of the farm. He also had worked for a short period during his teen years and early twenties as a weaver in the Delavan knitting mills. There he had learned a knitter's knot, one so small and tight that it could pass through a machine's needle. Years later, with great pride, he taught the knitter's knot to his sons.

As a young man, Earl heard from the neighbors tales of his father's youth and good times. His father, who had owned one of the first Model Ts in Sugar Creek, grew weary of the sporting life and settled into farming after a near-fatal skid on an Indian motorcycle on a gravel road. After the harvest in the fall of 1924, he and his good friend Mervin Kittleson set out in the Ford for California. They worked along the way to pay their expenses, finally hooking up with a California Power and Light Company crew to build towers for high-power electricity. The two were home for the spring planting. The images of their trip remain stored in the veneer music cabinet on the front porch of the farmhouse. After the Second World War, Earl's father occasionally talked about selling out and opening a hamburger shop in town: something that would put him in Delavan and in contact with other people.

•

Earl's mother, Alice Marie, grew up on a farm north of Millard in a remote, sparsely settled farming area. The only child of William Holloway and Lorena Taylor, she had a lonely early life. In an old photograph she stands alone on a snow-covered hill beside the South Side Heart Prairie School. Her mother died of Bright's disease when Alice Marie was thirteen years old. She and her father remained on the farm for several years before moving to a house in Millard. From there she would go to the high school in Elkhorn. Eventually she attended the State Normal School in Whitewater and then taught the eight grades in the Bay Hill School, a rural school near Williams Bay. It was during these school-teaching years that she met and married Floyd Quinney.

Her family was English on both sides. Her maternal great-grandfather, George Taylor, was a cabinetmaker and carpenter who designed and built several handsome Greek Revival farmhouses that still stand in LaGrange Township, Walworth County, where the family prospered as farmers. On her father's side, the Holloways had been small tenant farmers on a lord's estate in Devon; they too had settled on a farm in Walworth County and, as her grandfather James Holloway's obituary put it in 1911, "by diligence and hard labor made it a fine place."

They were country people, all of them, and their roots went deep into the Walworth County soil. Alice Marie's aunt Lizzie, who lived to be ninety-eight, spent nearly all her adult life on the farm across the field to the west of the Quinney place. Looking across the field toward evening, Earl would watch the sun set over his aunt Lizzie's farm. Before he was three, he had found a way through the fence and across the field to her house where he spent many afternoons throughout his boyhood.

"Will," as Earl's grandfather W. V. B. Holloway was known, was regarded early in his life as one of the most progressive of Sugar Creek's younger farmers. The children and grandchildren of his contemporaries remember him as the township clerk, an elective position he held for fifty-six years. He was a loyal Republican all his life. Earl could remember his grandfather arguing with Julius Johnson, one of Sugar Creek's few Democrats, late into the night, long after the fact, about Roosevelt's New Deal.

Later in his life, Will would sit at his desk in his house working on township business. In a photograph published by the *Elkhorn Enterprise* to accompany an article commemorating his many years of clerking for Sugar Creek, he is shown sitting at his desk, a plat map of the county stretched out in front of him. Around his hand is a rubber band he used to hold up the sleeve of his dress shirt. His green visor, worn to shield the light from the lamp, rests on the desk. A wooden telephone, with two bells on top and a pencil on a string dangling from the voicepiece, hangs on the wall behind him.

Earl and his brother spent many Saturday nights with Grandpa Will and his wife, Mabel, in their house. The evening always ended with a bowl of popcorn, which, as his grandfather said, was "good for a weekly cleaning out of the insides." Each evening, Grandpa Will walked to the corner store in Millard to pick up the newspaper. As he walked home at dusk one February evening in his eighty-sixth year, he was killed, in front of his house, by a drunk driver.

Floyd and Alice Quinney continued to work the long, hard hours on the farm. Their life together spanned from the early years of the 1930s to the late 1960s. The nature of farming changed rapidly in their later years. They barely kept up with the latest farming techniques as agriculture moved from family farming to agribusiness. As they got older and their sons moved away, they gradually reduced their farm work, avoiding the necessary but expensive changes they could not afford.

Earl's parents came to visit him and his family in New York City when Floyd Quinney was in his sixty-ninth year. Sitting around the dinner table on the final night of their visit, Floyd solemnly told everyone gathered there that the end was not far off for him. "I take the medicine that the doctor prescribes for my heart," he said, "but sometimes my heart flutters." Immediately everyone tried to brush away what had just been said, as if to brush crumbs off the tablecloth. "No," Earl had insisted, "you're going to live for a long time."

Two weeks later, back on the farm in Wisconsin, Floyd stopped his tractor after hauling a load of corn up from the fields. It was a cold November afternoon. He went into the metal shed to repair something from the tractor and fell dead of a heart attack beside the workbench. Alice found him a couple of hours later when she returned from grocery shopping in town.

Earl's father had tried to tell his son that he knew he was going to die soon, that he wanted help in facing that certainty. Earl felt—not for the first time—that he had failed his father. Now his father was gone. But the land of his father, and of all those who had gone before, was calling him more strongly than ever.

•

As a child, Earl had been an intimate part of the landscape whose woods and fields and sky measured the depth and breadth of his existence. Standing on a hill, he would look toward the far ridges along the horizon and know the immensity of the world. The landscape of the farm had been a source of inspiration all his life.

One day, when Earl was eight years old, he walked along the cow path east of the barn, on the side of the hill that ran down to the woods. He lay down on his back in the pasture grass and looked up into the sky. Coming out of the clouds, in many colors, appeared an image— the face of George Washington. Earl was struck with surprise and then with awe. It occurred to him that he had been singled out for something unusual. Good works must follow this privileged experience. He had been chosen.

This mysterious feeling of awe and wonder and purpose was part of his early years in the country school. Dunham School, District Number 9, was a one-room building of red brick that stood on an acre of land surrounded by giant American elms. The girls' outhouse was along the south fence in back of the school; the boys' outhouse, to the north. A baseball diamond occupied the rest of the yard. Looking out toward the west, beyond the fields and woods, Earl could see the farm. Inside the one-room school, a world was being created.

Getting to school in the morning and returning home at the end of the day were part of the adventure of school. Most days of the year, Earl and Ralph either walked or rode their bicycles to and from school. When walking, they took the gravel road, the longer distance, or cut across the fields and through the woods. The family album contains several photographs taken the first day of each school year: Earl and Ralph poised at their bicycles, sometimes with one leg thrown over the bar, ready for the ride to school.

Halfway up the winding road, they stopped each morning to pick up the Gies kids, Betty and

Jim. From there on, the journey to school was affected by the seasons of the year. On bright fall days, the last of the goldenrod and sumac marked their way. Later, migrating ducks and geese made their calls flying overhead. In early spring, following the long winter, water flowed beneath cracking ice and hardened snow, making perilous the passage over ditches along the sides of the road. One year in late spring, they sang all the way to school, "O What a Beautiful Mornin'."

It was the winter, however, that furnished the children with the greatest adventures of travel to and from school. There were days of walking in knee-deep snow, and arduous journeys through the stark, silent woods. The highlight of travel was to ride the bobsleigh. A snowfall of two or three feet meant that the milkman would not be able to make it down the road to the farm. Earl's father would have to get the cans of milk up to the main road, a distance of over a mile. He would hitch the two white work horses to the long bobsleigh and would load in the milk cans. Earl and Ralph would pile in; their father, dressed in his sheepskin coat, would take the reins; and with the breath steaming from the horses' nostrils, they would make their way to the main road. They often had to stop to shovel their way through the deep drifts. On other days, if the snowplow had already cleared the road, they would glide over the packed snow with great style in the one-horse cutter, sleigh bells ringing all the way to school.

Arriving at school, the children would place their winter coats and boots in the front vestibule, put their lunch pails on the shelf, and sometimes, before sitting down to work, would make a treat for their winter lunch: snow mousse. Into a metal container they would pour a mixture of sugar, chocolate syrup, eggs, and cream, and then bury it outside in the snow. At noon the mousse would be ready for dessert.

And then one morning, spring would finally come to Dunham School. Memories of those days abound, but a typical day might show Skeeter Duesterbeck coming down the paved road in front of the school, his wagon loaded with fresh drinking water for the day. Earl and Pat McDonald, being assigned the daily task of putting out the flag, run the flag up the pole in the front yard of the school. The children settle into their desks, placing books and tablets in the compartments under their desk tops. Throughout the day, each grade, consisting of two or three students, takes its turn as a class in the front of the room. The rest of the children continue with their studies, listening much of the time to their teacher, Miss Roekcr, and to their friends reciting their lessons. They learn from those who are younger, at a point where they have once been, and from those who are older and more advanced in their studies. Eight grades of students are learning together.

During those years, at 10:30 every Monday morning, the teacher turned on the radio to WHA, the state educational station in Madison. This was the morning for "Afield with Ranger Mac." Wakelin McNeel, with all the wonder in his voice, broadcast this program on the Wisconsin School of the Air for twenty years to children in the rural schools. "Come along, boys and girls," he would say; and "the trailhitters" would be off with Ranger Mac, exploring the marshes, walking the edge of a farm creek, or entering a northern pine forest. They learned about the earth's natural resources and the changing signs of the seasons and the intimate joys of being attuned to the world of nature. Ranger Mac ended each program: "And until next week, may the Great Spirit put sunshine in your heart today and forever more, heap much."

In the back of the schoolroom was the museum. A dark oak cabinet with glass doors, it contained the artifacts of nature and the wonders of earthly habitation. Collected on walks to and from school were Indian arrowheads, snake skins, the skull of a skunk, all kinds of rocks, jars of powdery substances, fungi and large mushrooms, strangely shaped twigs, a turtle shell, and decaying objects gathered long ago but too precious to discard. Years later, Earl would wonder what had happened to the specimens after Dunham School had closed for the last time in the 1950s, a casualty of school consolidation.

Two recesses a day, plus the noon hour, gave the farm children time for play. Fall and spring were times for baseball games, boys and girls teaming together on a baseball field well worn from seventy-five years of play. The old merry-go-round turned most of the time during recess, sometimes swinging back and forth until it nearly fell off its center pole. Dividing into sides, the children played Andy-Over-the-School-House, tagging each other to increase their team size as the game progressed. One warm spring day, with the smell of peanut butter and jam sandwiches still hanging in the noontime air, they built a grass house over fallen branches. (Some older students later boasted about doing unusual things in the dark of the grass house.)

One particularly cold and dark March afternoon, all the students were skating on the pond beyond the fence in the field of the Duesterbeck farm. Earl was feeling cold and devilish. He yelled across the ice to Bob Duesterbeck, who was making a turn on the other side of the pond: "Bob loves Pearl!" This immediately caught Bob's attention. He skated toward Earl at a fast clip and threw him down on the ice. Earl's leg broke sharply in two places. Carefully tended by his mother, Earl spent the next six weeks at home on the sofa. On dark winter days for years to come, his aching leg reminded him of Bob and Pearl and the love he attributed to them.

The following winter provided the children with a memorable Christmas program. The schoolroom was lavishly decorated with a colored Nativity scene chalked on the blackboard and construction paper figures pinned to the wallboard around the room. At the completion of the evening's Christmas program of stories, skits, recitations, and musical numbers, Santa Claus appeared with the slam of the front door and the ringing of sleigh bells. The children and the adults knew that year's Santa as the farmer up the road from the school, the man who drank too much. After handing out the presents, Santa concluded his lively appearance by engaging both the young and the old in a contest. With the room divided in half, he instructed everyone to see which side could sing "Silent Night" louder. The irony of the event was not lost on anyone by the time the shouting neared its end. Into the winter night went children and parents, with "Silent Night" literally ringing in their ears.

Following the spring planting and before the beginning of the summer haying season, the annual Dunham School picnic marked the ending of the school year. Before the picnic dinner began, the children and the adults enjoyed a game of baseball, while the old-timers reminisced in small groups around the school yard. Earl was busy taking around the autograph book that he had started during the school year, trying to get each page filled by the end of the day. His classmate Mary Balogh presented him with an autograph that read: "You had a little lamp, very well trained no doubt. Every time your girlfriend comes, the little lamp goes out." Ending the verse, she added, "Yours till Niagara falls." Jimmy Gies wrote: "When you see a monkey up in the tree, just pull his tail and think of me." The neighbor man Burton Hanson, who was a close friend to Earl, wrote: "Remember me when far, far off, where the woodchucks die with the whooping cough."

During one of her visits to the school in 1946, the country school superintendent, Ella Jacobson, summarized what learning meant for Earl, both at Dunham School and in subsequent years when learning became not only his work but also his happiness:

Dear Earl,
Every time I visit this school I find you doing good work. Always do your very best in everything you do. This will bring you success, and you will be happy in your work.

In the spring of 1947, the end of Earl's seventh grade, only five students remained at Dunham School. The school had to be closed until there were more students. Earl completed the eighth grade at Island School in Richmond Township. He and Ralph would walk west through fields and woods to reach the school. That year, for the first time in his life, Earl felt the painful reality of change. The transfer to Island School marked the beginning of a move from home.

Maybe the problem was one of age—of being thirteen years old—rather than one of change. Earl liked his eighth-grade teacher, Miss Helling, very much. But human relations took on a new character. There was both a competitiveness and a hardness in playing with others that he had not previously encountered. Baseball games had become a trial of one's strength and agility. Being selected for Mr. Baker's basketball team required a test of one's athletic ability. Play was now a threatening experience. Earl was both bewildered and overwhelmed when another boy asked an unheard-of question: "Why don't you show me yours?"

The eighth grade finally drew to an end. Earl was selected from candidates from all the grade schools in Richmond Township to deliver the commencement speech. At the countywide commencement, held in Lake Geneva, Earl prepared to deliver his carefully researched speech on the early settlers of Richmond Township. Dressed in new trousers and his first sport coat, he began

to speak, and at the same time his new trousers began to darken. In excitement and fear, he had wet his pants.

•

After a summer of working in the fields, Earl began high school. The four years of Delavan High School marked a period of departure from the life of the farm. He never completed the leave-taking, although he lived those years trying to move away from the farm, believing that he had to sever all ties to the ways of life on the farm. Removing the farm from his life would never be possible, but as a teenager, he did not know this.

Although he had not reached the legal driving age when he began high school, he obtained a special driver's permit, and his parents allowed him to use the pickup truck to drive the five miles to the high school. Driving into town in the truck and searching for a parking place near the school let everyone know that he was from the farm. His clothes had the look of country, although he tried to dress like the town kids. On his mind much of the time was the difference between the students who had grown up in town and those who had grown up on the farm. But rather than define their rural character with some distinction and pride, the students from the farm accepted their assigned second-class citizenship and tried to become more like the town students.

During his second year in high school, Earl's difficulties in making the transition to town became more acute. He developed sharp stomach pains that made getting to school a trial each morning. The pain finally settled in his right side—the obvious sign of appendicitis. Dr. Crowe agreed with Earl's persistent self-diagnosis. The appendix must come out. Following the operation, the doctor placed the appendix in a jar and studied it. There was no inflammation; he had removed a perfectly good appendix.

But somehow Earl began to feel better, and after the operation and recovery, he returned to school with new confidence.

He threw himself into extracurricular activities to prove his worth both to himself and to others. His classes were going well, but he noticed that students became known by their accomplishments outside class. Sports were out for him; he lacked the skills that come with years of practice, and besides, he had to get home right after school to do chores on the farm. Instead, Earl became photographer for the high school newspaper. He photographed school events, football and basketball games, plays, and teachers, and he made candid shots in the hallways. On stormy nights, he traveled to Lake Geneva, Walworth, and McHenry to cover the games. With Lee Farrar and Terry Itnyre, he wrote the stories, finding twenty-five different verbs, including "whips," "trounces," "bows to," and "licks," to headline the results of a game and carefully avoiding verbs like "wins" and "defeats". He learned to develop and print film, and each week one of his photographs appeared on the front page of the *Spotlight*.

He received a good review for his part in *The Ugly Duckling*. "He shows promise," the reviewer in the town newspaper wrote. It was his first and last part in a play; but during the months of rehearsals, he had gotten to know the town students better. And they had begun to pay some attention to him. The high point came for Earl when Bill Hodge invited him to come over to his house with other town kids to watch General MacArthur on television deliver his "old soldiers never die" speech to the United States Congress. Earl was beginning to make it in town.

At the beginning of first year of high school, Earl decided that he would play in the high school band. He selected the trombone, and though he had never held one before, he knew it was the right instrument for him. With some of his pig-raising money, he purchased a new silver trombone. It went with him through college, where he also played in the band. In graduate school and into his second year of marriage, he took the trombone to the radio store near the state capitol in Madison and told the dealer that he wanted to trade it for an FM radio. The dealer said, "Are you certain you want to do this? You'll never have the money to buy another trombone." And for a long time, the dealer was right.

Earl learned to play the trombone in lessons given to him by Mr. Kleyensteuber, the band director. Soon he was in the band among the trombones. The band marched at the games, put on concerts, and made trips throughout southeastern Wisconsin. In the clarinet section sat Peggy Starin, who became Earl's high school sweetheart. She was his first love, one that brought him distrustful glances and censorious comments from his mother. Peggy followed him to college the year after he graduated from high school. With his sights on graduate school and an uncharted career, along with her desire for a more dependable partner, they eventually parted company.

During Earl's third year in high school, he formed a dance band that played at school dances. On one occasion, with crepe paper streamers hanging from the ceiling of the gym, the lights turned low, and one hundred couples dancing in each other's arms, the band worked its magic. Grayson Babcock, with the mellowest and saddest sound ever heard on a saxophone, took the lead on "Little White Lies." In the spotlight, Earl stood up and played his rendition of "Stardust." The repertoire continued with "Five Foot Two, Eyes of Blue," "I'm in the Mood for Love," and "Pennies from Heaven." As the Harvest Dance came to an end at midnight, the dance band played its closing number,

"I'll See You in My Dreams." Afterward, Peggy and Earl went out into the starry night.

Earl's days in the Delavan High School marching band were concluded at the end of his senior year with the Memorial Day parade. Following tradition, the marching band led the parade down the main street. Units of the American Legion, veterans of the two world wars, followed, wearing uniforms long outgrown and carrying guns over their shoulders to mark the meaning of the day. Local riders on nervous horses added a bit of glamour and excitement. The parade ended on the hill at the Spring Grove Cemetery, where paraders and townspeople gathered around the memorial monument to Delavan's war dead. A small man, assigned the task each year, climbed unsteadily up the monument and placed a wreath over the top. The lead trumpet player discreetly withdrew from the band and placed himself behind the hill to play a muted version of "Taps." Then the band broke ranks, and the musicians walked back to the school to change out of their uniforms. With the other graduating seniors, Earl said his good-byes and departed, wondering what was to come next.

•

To Earl, the 1940s really began with an announcement on the radio in the late afternoon of a cold December Sunday in 1941. Floyd and Alice Quinney were sitting in the living room with their feet propped close to the hot-air register. Earl and Ralph were sitting on the sofa, their work clothes on, waiting to start the evening chores. The program was interrupted: Pearl Harbor had been bombed. A new era was beginning.

All the years of growing up had been years of farming the land. Farming was the way the family made a living. Life on the farm meant work for everyone. School and play and other adventures took place only after work was done.

In the 1940s, the very nature of farming was changing, just as Earl was changing. By the time of his high school graduation, a new form of agriculture had evolved. The family farm would never be the same.

The Quinney family, like so many families around them, were experiencing the last days of a passing way of life. Electricity had arrived in the mid-1930s. The windmill that had once pumped water from the well had been dismantled. The Delco light plant with its liquid-filled batteries in the basement of the house was used only when the electrical power failed because of an ice storm. Milking machines that allowed a larger number of cows to be milked faster than by hand were installed in the barn. A newer model Oliver tractor replaced the old one, and a combine replaced the grain binder and threshing machine. The tongue on the horse-drawn hay mower was sawed off and replaced with a new hitch to accommodate the tractor.

But despite these changes, the ways of the Quinney family seemed to belong to a former world. They still felt like simple people. They were still small-time farmers, country people, "hicks" in comparison to townspeople. Earl's feelings became mixed: He did not want to grow away from his parents, but at the same time, he wanted to become modern. He could not separate his attitude toward the farm from the one he felt toward his parents.

In August 1945, the war with Japan ended. An atomic bomb killed two hundred thousand people on the other side of the world. The people of Walworth County celebrated victory in the streets of Elkhorn. After finishing the chores and the milking by 6:00 P.M., the earliest hour ever in their farming history, Earl, Ralph, and their mother and father dressed and drove to Elkhorn. They had to park on the outskirts of town because so many people had arrived to celebrate. Bud Count, who had taken the boys swimming often during the war years, was at the drums, leading his band for the dancing in the streets. Shortly before midnight, the Quinneys made their way to the car and home again. In later years, Earl could not remember if he felt anticipation of a new world or relief in the passing of the old one, but he did remember sensing that something in the lives of his family and in their world would never again be the same.

The daily farm chores, always tied closely to the weather and to the passage of the seasons, went on as usual. Each season brought with it tasks that had to be completed before another season began. The farmer and his sons prepared for the necessary labors and attuned themselves to the requirements of changing form and pace. Their spirits ebbed and flowed with the seasons.

Though winter was a time for allowing the land to slumber under its cover of snow, work continued on the farm. There were maintenance repairs on buildings and machinery and always the daily chores of milking the cows and caring for and feeding the farm animals. During the coldest part of winter, as icicles grew longer each day along the eaves of the barn, farm animals wandered outside only at the warmest time on a sunny day.

Of all the winter chores, the morning milkings were especially trying. Always, endlessly, there were the early morning risings in the cold to milk the cows. Putting on long underwear in the dark and walking through snow drifts, the Quinney men would make their way to the barn. The cows would get up from their stalls, their breath filling the musty air. Cats, lazy after the night's sleep, would leave their beds under the straw to welcome the men. The great Holstein bull in the heavily barred stall at the end of the barn would bellow a morning greeting. As Earl and Ralph strapped the milking machines to the first two cows, placing the cold milk cups on their four teats and turning on the valve above the stanchion, the milking would begin for another morning.

On the mornings when the electricity had gone out because of a storm, they milked the cows using pressure produced by the gasoline-powered generator. If the engine would not start, they were forced to milk the entire herd by hand, not just the old cows and the hard-teaters that required milking by hand every day. Earl's father would sit on the wooden stool with his head against a cow's body to do the hand milking. On other days, a small black radio tuned to WLS would bring news and music to break the sounds of the animals and the milking machines.

An April breeze signaled a warming of the land. A heavy snowfall might still come well into May, but as the sun grew brighter and as geese were seen flying in formation toward their northern homes, people knew that winter was ending. This was the time when farmers could enjoy the pleasure of going to town every day. They could order baby chickens at the hatchery, purchase seed corn and grain at the mill, and take plowshares to the blacksmith. Earl liked to accompany his father to the blacksmith's shop, where he would stand in the darkened room and watch fire and sparks fly from the forge as the blacksmith pounded a hard new edge into red-hot shares.

With spring came the time for the farm animals to give birth. By the end of March, Earl's father would make nightly trips to the pig house. When birth was certain to take place, his father would spend the entire night watching over the sows. (Without tending, the old sows might roll over onto the new litter, crushing some of the young.) The lambs were born without trouble, their mothers sometimes giving birth in the snow. The Quinneys always felt joy in the lambing of twins. Newborn calves received special attention because of their size and their economic importance to the farm. The veterinarian, Dr. Anderson, made trips to the farm in advance of their births to detect potential problems. If he examined a cow and discovered that the calf's hooves pointed in the wrong direction, he could expect a call at his home in Elkhorn alerting him that delivery was imminent. To save the life of the calf and often that of the mother, he would be forced to reach into the mother and pull out the calf. Many of the calves grew to become milking cows. Earl took care not to become attached to the calves that were destined to be shipped each fall to the Milwaukee stockyards.

Dr. Anderson had come from Greeley, Colorado, to Walworth County during the Great Depression to start his practice. He was still a man of the West when Earl knew him. On one of his calls to the farm, he gave Earl a lariat that he had brought from Colorado. The lariat, a fifteen-foot rope made of the finest pliable sisal with a brass thimble braided into the end, became one of Earl's prized possessions. With great care, Dr. Anderson taught Earl how to use the lariat, how to twirl it in a wide loop to land the noose around the neck of a calf or cow. Later, when he became really good at using the lariat, Earl would ride his horse, Sparkplug, to the hidden end of the pasture to single out a cow to rope and bring back to the barn.

The frogs in the pond down at the old place heralded the arrival of spring. Their croaking and peeping sounded clearly in the evenings when the days grew warmer. The redwinged blackbirds returned to the pond, the males perching on top of cattails from the previous year. They scolded loudly, establishing their territory for the mating and nesting that would soon follow. Three or four mallards spent the night along the edge of the pond. Tadpoles began to swim in the shallows, and grasses shot up green all around the pond. The red buds on the silver maples appeared ready to open. There were many wonders of spring in sight, but little time to linger to observe them. Spring brought work to be done on the farm.

Some of the fields had been plowed during the fall before the snows came. The soft,

moist soil in these fields was ready for tilling. The other fields needed to be plowed and disked, and corn stalks and oat stubble needed to be turned. At the beginning of preparing the fields, the soil turned to mud, sticking to the cleats on the huge rear tires of the tractor and dropping off in the driveway as the tractor was driven back from the field. Gradually the land dried in the warm sun, and dust would rise as the fields were worked. Earl and Ralph would hurry home from school each afternoon to complete the dragging and disking of the Quinney land. Looking over the hood of the green tractor as he pulled the drag from one end of the field to the other, Earl would feel small against the long horizon. He would sing at the top of his voice as he whirled the steering wheel with the palm of his hand on the ball of the spinner knob to begin another round.

The Quinneys planted oats first, pulling the grain drill back and forth over the smooth fields and stopping after each round to refill the oat and fertilizer compartments. They would plant corn next, and by the end of May, they would see green tips of corn emerging from the warm soil planted only two weeks earlier with tiny seeds. With planting completed, Floyd Quinney and his sons would rest a bit from their labors and wait for the alfalfa, clover, and timothy to mature.

By June the hay was ready for its first cutting. The smell of freshly cut clover would spread over the fields as bees buzzed about gathering pollen. As the hay was cut, it would fall into neat rows behind the mower. Sometimes this would end tragically when the harsh mower blade cut off the legs of a young rabbit. After allowing the hay to lie in the fields for a day or two to dry, the Quinneys would stack the wagon high with hay. Inevitably some of it would drop from the hayloader as it was drawn behind the wagon across the fields. After pulling the wagon to the barn, the farmer and his sons would unload the hay into the mow.

Following the haying season came long days of cutting and binding the grain. The tasks for Earl and Ralph included running the grain binder. They would hitch the McCormick-Deering binder, which had once been pulled by two horses, to the Oliver tractor. All day long, the boys—Ralph on the binder adjusting the levers of the cutting blade and releasing the bundles, Earl driving the tractor—would move across the oat field. Earl wore a dust mask, outfitted with a penlight battery, to alleviate his hay fever, caused by the dusty grain. Each year from the time he was seven or eight years old, he would complain to his father that he was being worked too hard. As he drove the tractor over rough and hilly fields, he had visions of kids in town playing and loafing while he worked all day long in the hot sun, sneezing his head off.

On one hot summer day, the binder broke down and had to be pulled in for repairs. Sitting on the lawn under the oak tree, Earl watched his father's attempts to fix the binder. He watched more closely as his father tried to pry loose a bolt with the new claw hammer that Earl had recently purchased. Growing more and more irritated at his father's efforts, which he found inept, and suddenly seeing the hardwood handle of his hammer snap in two, Earl shouted, "You're the dumbest man I know! I'm so much smarter than you! I don't belong on the farm!" For many years, Earl remembered his outburst as the Hammer Incident, and he regretted his harsh words and the visible pain he had caused his father.

At the end of the summer, the threshing machine, owned and worked cooperatively with several farm neighbors, was pulled into the field and placed south of the barn. One of Earl's favorite photographs, taken by his mother with the family's Kodak box camera, showed the threshing machine, powered by the old tractor turning the long, twisted belt, blowing straw in the air into the growing stack. One man was

on the horse-drawn wagon, pitching grain bundles into the hopper of the thresher; another stood atop the enormous machine, tending the threshed oats. A white leghorn hen stood in the lower left-hand corner of the picture.

Threshing time depended on the readiness of each farmer's crop of grain. When the Quinney's grain was threshed, it was the responsibility of Earl's mother to prepare and serve the noon meal to the threshing crew. Several farm wives would come to help her with the large dinner on the two or three days that the crew worked the Quinney farm; she would return the help when the crew moved on to another farm. Promptly at noon, the power belt from the tractor would be released and the machine would fall silent. The load of grain bundles remaining on the wagon would wait until after the noon hour. The horses would be placed in a shady spot, given water, and their feed bags attached.

The metal-frame washstands, complete with Lava soap and towels, would be set up in the back yard. After each thresher washed, immersing his face in the white enamel pan, the water was thrown out and fresh water was poured for the next man. The workers seated themselves on the back porch at the oak table whose extra leaves had been added, along with additional leaves borrowed from a neighbor, to make a place for everyone. The food would arrive: mashed potatoes, meat, and gravy, followed by hot apple pie and chunks of cheddar cheese for dessert. The smoothness of the mashed potatoes would establish the quality of the meal. Earl's mother would receive compliments from the well-fed crew, some of whom would wander off to finish the hour with a short nap under the Chinese elms.

The threshing season came right before the Walworth County Fair, and usually threshing was completed before the fair began. To complete the threshing was important because summer's grand finale was the fair, a time to show the livestock and farm products that had been attended to all during the spring and summer. At the county fair, Earl would show the pigs he had been raising all summer. His pigs were not ordinary pigs, but purebred Duroc hogs. By raising purebreds, all with certified registration papers, he avoided selling his pigs for pork at the end of the season. His pigs were either sold as breeding stock or retained another year as his own breeding stock. At the fair, he would hang out a painted wooden sign to promote his purebred Duroc hogs.

His enterprise—all planned from the beginning—had the objective and result of providing him with the money for his college education. An ordinary fattened pig would sell for about fifty dollars in the winter after nine months of slopping and feeding, but purebreds might bring three hundred fifty dollars. Moreover, if some of his pigs won prizes at the county fair in September, he would be assured of particularly good sales. When Earl finally entered Carroll College, he did not disclose to his fellow students the source of his financing.

The unstated attraction of the county fair was being able to be away from home for several days. Earl spent the nights sleeping in a big tent with other 4-H members. During the day, he would roam the fairgrounds unattended and uninhibited. It was a time to greet neighbors on a new territory. Grandfather Will was always in the Agriculture Building looking at the prize seed corn and vegetables. Farmers sat on and walked around the latest improvements in machinery. Neighbors picnicked on the green, listening to the band. Others viewed horse races and special acts from the grandstand. Earl would stop often to listen to western music being played in the tent operated by the Janesville radio station WCLO. Food was abundant: Harold Loomer's hamburgers, the Bethel Church hotdogs, Willard Olson's pronto pups, and peanut-covered ice-cream bars.

In the recesses of the imagination, there is something darkly exotic about a carnival, and the Midwest carnivals were no different. They seemed both a source of magic and mystery, as well as a source of fear. Farmers for generations kept their wives and children from the woods beyond the fairgrounds where the carnival workers encamped. They feared that the women and children would disappear along with the gypsy-like characters that they saw once a year.

For Earl, though, the carnival meant excitement, and he looked forward each year to being caught up in the sounds, vibrant colors, and crowds of the carnival. On the midway, he would see strange-looking men and women beckoning: a woman in tight pants offering darts for popping balloons; a man, with tattooed arms and an open shirt, holding out three balls to knock down a stack of wooden milk bottles. Walking past a tent with an arcade of machines, he could hear wild noises and see people wandering out with cards dispensed for a penny. Other sights would draw him on: two-headed reptiles, dwarfed men, and bearded ladies; motorcycles roaring inside a rickety-walled inverted dome; revolving wooden animals and dragons painted orange, teal, and red; an octopus-shaped ride ablaze with colored lights reaching up and out into the night sky. And, of course, there was the Ferris wheel. It was always wonderful, especially the time when Earl, having waited a year to ask her, finally sat at the top with Kate Seymour.

The county fair did not mean the end of the year's harvesting. The work, however, seemed easy compared to that of the summer, partly because Earl and Ralph had returned to the refuge of school. Earl's father would spend his days cutting ripe corn, hauling it to the silo-filler, and blowing the chopped corn into the cement silo. After days of fermenting, the chopped corn would turn into silage for the winter feeding of the cows. When the best corn had completely ripened into hard kernels, it was picked by hand, ear by ear, and thrown into the waiting wagon alongside the rows. The wagon was then unloaded, the large golden ears of corn going into permanent cribs and snow fence cribs constructed to hold the overflow.

After the fall harvesting, when winter had set in, Earl's father took care of other aspects of farming, such as equipment maintenance or selling livestock. Taking livestock to market was exciting, for it meant a day away from the monotony of farm life. On one cold gray winter's day when Earl was twelve, his father allowed him to stay home from school to go with him to take a load of pigs to market in Milwaukee. Like most children who get to go on personal trips on school days, Earl looked forward to the trip for many days. Going away with his father made him feel grown up.

As he helped his father drive the squealing pigs up the ramp attached to the black Chevy truck, Earl had to keep telling himself that taking pigs to market was part of farming. It was difficult to separate himself and his emotional attachment to the animals from the realities of farm life. When the pigs were loaded, and after he waved good-bye to his mother, he turned his attention to the trip.

They drove the sixty miles to the Cudahy stockyards in Milwaukee in a seemingly short time. There at the stockyards, Earl and his father watched as their pigs were unloaded, weighed, and driven through the wooden gates to their destination. After the pigs were sold, Earl and his father walked up the stairway to the dining hall where farmers in manure-covered overalls were gathering for lunch. They joined other farmers to sit at a long table for their meal of hot sliced roast beef, mashed potatoes, creamy gravy, with bread and butter and coffee on the side.

Later, on the drive back home, Earl watched from his window as they passed through low-lying farmland where muskrat houses dotted every pond and marsh and yellow-branched willow trees lined the banks of the creeks. Looking through the wintry haze, he wondered how other people lived their lives, and he thought of the experiences of this day as ones that he would always remember. Soon they had driven the sixty miles to the farm, just in time to begin the evening chores.

•

In the years between 1940 and 1952, life moved between school, play, and farm work, each activity shaping the others. But Earl's lasting impression was of his profound desire to fill his life with something other than farm work. His father would continuously ask his mother, "Why doesn't that boy want to work?" Earl's most pleasant memories were of things that found a place outside farming, of time left over when farm work was completed or interrupted.

On summer evenings, after the cows had been milked, Earl and Ralph would jump on their bicycles and head into the sunset. Earl would be on the Silver King that he had bought used on a farm near Darien and that, with its enormous shock absorber on the front column just above the wheel, made riding easy on even the roughest terrain. They would play out the Lone Ranger and Tonto adventures that they had heard on the radio while doing their chores. They would ride west in the direction of their aunt Lizzie's hayfield in a quest of good against the forces of evil. His imaginary silver bullets blazing into the sky, Earl always knew that his world was wider than a dairy farm in the Midwest.

The highlight of the week would come when Earl's father had to go to town for repairs or to purchase supplies. The boys were disappointed when they had to stay home to complete their chores or continue the planting or harvesting. But their father did not impose this restraint often, and he usually allowed the boys to go to town with him. He enjoyed the trips to town as much as they did.

Trips to the feed mill in town were always preceded by loading the truck with corn and oats to be ground into feed for the cows, pigs, sheep, and chickens. Once at the mill in Elkhorn, Earl and Ralph would wander around the mill buildings and end up in the office, watching and listening to talk that they did not hear at home. Their mother would go to the meat locker to get enough pork and beef from the freezer to last the week. When a hog had recently been butchered and processed, there would be buckets of lard to take home for use in cooking and baking. Stopping for a snack on the way home completed an afternoon in town.

Earl's father was not a talkative man, and frequently he seemed uncomfortable with other people, although his demeanor in no way reflected a preference for avoiding human contact. His awkwardness stemmed, instead, from the feeling of backwardness that farmers sense in themselves in the presence of others, especially townspeople. One bright summer morning, on a trip to town to get something at the hardware store, he greeted a townsman with an unusually verbose display of heartiness. Afterward, as if in explanation or apology, he looked down at Earl and said, "Always give a friendly hello to people you meet on the street. It shows that you are a good person and that you care about others."

On Sundays the family would go to the Delavan Methodist Church. The boys were sent to Sunday school and were then expected to be present at the eleven o'clock church service, which their parents generally attended. Sitting beside his mother and father, Earl would wonder what religion meant to them. Neither of his parents sang the hymns, and his mother did not even seem to close her eyes when the prayers were given. The boys were taken faithfully to all the church activities. But instead of gaining any particular belief, some doctrine that could be believed in with confidence, Earl privately acquired a habit of wondering about the mysteries of the world. Those mysteries absorbed much of his creative imagination, and to him they became important and necessary, a basis for a commitment to discover and appreciate the obscurities of the world.

When he was younger, Earl often asked his mother to read the Bible to him at bedtime. She would hesitate, as if embarrassed, and then suggest that some other reading might be more appropriate as bedtime reading. Perhaps she thought a terror of the unknown was too much to face in the hour before sleep. Instead, she would bring out *The Rover Boys at School*, a book given to Earl one Christmas by his uncle Lloyd and his aunt Elsie. It would do. It was the story of three brothers left fatherless and sent away to boarding school. The oldest brother, Richard, was "tall and slender, with dark eyes and dark hair. He was a rather quiet boy, one who loved to read and study, although he was not above having a good time now and then, when he felt like breaking loose." The book was filled with the adventures of the brothers away from home, and Earl never tired of it.

Home was a virtuous territory. This meant the exclusion of everything that had to do with the unknown and unexplored region of sexuality. Anything of this nature was a surprise and meant trouble or embarrassment for everyone concerned. Measures to avoid such embarrassment were usually taken, but there were times when it could not be avoided. Such was the case when Earl and several friends were rafting down at the pond in the woods and a neighbor girl's bib overalls slipped to one side as she fell off a raft. That brief exposure brought as much embarrassment to Earl and the other onlookers as it did to the girl.

Even the suggestion of the feminine form

was enough to provoke embarrassment. Out in the barn stood his aunt Kate's shapely dress form, and though it was headless and mute, a mere representation of the feminine form, it was capable of arousing strange feelings in the adolescent farm boy. On one occasion, Earl explored uncharted territory. He took a neighbor girl, Jean, into the tent that he had constructed beside the house, and the two of them innocently lay together on the canvas cot. His mother discovered them when she pulled away the flap door of the tent to peer in. She gave him cold stares and severe looks for the next two days. By the time Earl attained the appropriate age for dating, it seemed that he had to break down heavy barriers to get enough courage to ask a girl for a date.

In nature and in the landscape, Earl gained some consolation and hope. His reconciliation with a life that was becoming more complex and mysterious was a gift brought to him by a neighbor, Burton Hanson. Sometime midway in the 1940s, Burton and his wife, Gladys, had moved from a rented farmhouse near Millard to the Dutcher place, the set of buildings and forty acres adjacent to the Quinney farm. Burton was to be the person who brought Earl close to nature. Next to parents and relatives, Burton became the most important adult in Earl's life. Occasionally Burton would take a trip north to the region where he had grown up, near Colby. Returning from one of the trips, he brought Earl a section of a fallen aspen tree he had sawed off, a section that had been chewed by a beaver. Forty years later, the beaver cutting still sits in Earl's bookcase.

Burton took Earl fishing many evenings after a long day of haying in the sun. Along Turtle Creek, he and Earl, usually with Earl's father and Ralph, fished for bullheads and sunfish. Catching the fish was only incidental to walking along the bank of the creek and waiting for the sun to set over the marsh. "Man alive," Bur-

ton would exclaim whenever someone caught a large fish or when a spectacular sunset lit up the evening sky. "Man alive!"

Burton had skills that were in short supply as the 1940s ended. He was a "handyman" who could repair or build just about anything. Neighbors sometimes questioned his workmanship, implying a series of mistakes in his work, but Burton would tell Earl: "Anyone can make something, but a good carpenter is one who can repair his mistakes." One summer Earl worked with Burton, and together they built a beautiful pig house on a farm north of Sharon.

The old farmhouse in which Burton and Gladys lived looked west to the far edge of the marsh to an oak knoll with two Indian mounds. Before the white settlers moved into southern Wisconsin, the area had been part of an Indian settlement, and their arrowheads were found when Earl's father plowed the field next to the wooded hill. There were stories that the mounds had been dug up at one time and that the disturbers had contracted numerous maladies. Burton would look longingly into the marsh and woods from his house on the hill.

Throughout the summer of 1948, Gladys lay in her bedroom, dying of cancer. Burton installed a buzzer at her bedside so that the bell that he placed outside her window would alert him if she needed help or comfort. Gone were the days when Gladys and Earl would play the Sunday prelude at the Millard Baptist Church, Gladys at the piano and Earl with either his trombone or his guitar. Gladys's condition worsened slowly, and she died at the end of that summer.

Although a few letters passed between them, Earl eventually lost contact with Burton. When he was a graduate student at Northwestern University, Earl had visited Burton once in a house in Maywood, a western suburb of Chicago where Burton would live the rest of his life. The last time Earl saw him was on the day of Floyd

Quinney's funeral. Burton had stood with the others for the brief moments at the graveside and afterward had retreated quickly to his waiting car parked over the hill. Though Earl had viewed him from a distance through falling snow, he could see the tears in Burton's eyes. They had not tried to speak to each other. There seemed to be no need.

•

When Earl returned to the farm in 1980, he suddenly felt himself part of a former time. He had grown up with the ideas and feelings he acquired from living on a Wisconsin dairy farm. His education in the rural schools of the 1940s continued to provide him with values. In all that he had learned on his journey, in all that he had accomplished in his lifetime, his memories of growing up on the farm most surely gave him his identity. As time passed, he had found himself drawn to the land of his birth. More than ever, he viewed himself as a part of nature and the landscape. Now he was beginning to find the source of his longing. He felt himself becoming a part of the natural world, a part of the farm. Every blade of grass, every organism, every force in the land seemed interrelated. His life on this planet was a part of nature. He would be remembered in the earth. The realization was not only sobering but also liberating.

One day during that visit in 1980, Earl and his mother drove the five miles to Delavan to do some laundry at the laundromat and to talk over a cup of coffee at the Travelers Coffee Shop. On the way, he asked her many questions about the past. He was trying to find parts of himself in her answers. But his questions bothered her; they filled her with emotions that made her uncomfortable and anxious.

Pointing to the right as they drove the familiar road to town, Earl asked, "Who used to live on that farm when I was growing up? I've forgotten."

His mother replied hesitantly, "I can't remember the name of the family. The farm has changed hands so many times."

Then the memories began to come back to him, and he remembered the main event associated with that farm: One summer evening in the late 1940s, a farmer new to the area was removing the rack from his truck to convert it into a pigpen. The jack slipped, and the rack fell on him, crushing him to death.

Every farm that Earl and his mother passed on the way to Delavan took on new meaning. On each place there had been one kind of tragedy or another. He remembered the joys of life—births, marriages, celebrations—but he most vividly recalled the tragedies.

He began to understand his mother's reaction to his questions about the past. For him, these events were being recalled after a long lapse of time and memory. But for her, they were a daily reality. Her daily world was charged with the emotions of a life lived for seventy-five years in the few miles around the farm. For her, forgetting about the past was one of the possible ways of living in the present. To recall the ghosts of family and friends and the associations they carried was to pay the price of living one's life all in one place. For years, Earl had escaped the past and some of the painful ways it can impinge on the present; but, as he had learned, no one can escape the past forever.

His flight from the place had been in part an attempt to find a force that would affirm life. In his years on the farm, he had developed an impulse that his academic colleagues would call "romantic." This had become his transport: a transcendence of the mundane world, a removal of himself from all that would deny the human spirit. In transcendence, divine or otherwise, he had traveled far beyond the circumscribed existence of rural Wisconsin. But in the process lay the contradiction and the tension; being uprooted, he was now in need of a home.

So he continued to walk the pastures and woodlots of the farm. He went down to the marsh where he had played so often when he was growing up. As he moved among the bogs and through thickets of quaking aspen, under a sky of startling blue, he sensed his oneness with nature and the enveloping universe. Swiftly summer was passing. Before long, the Indian mounds and muskrat houses would be blanketed in snow. Spring would return, and life would renew itself in the woods and marshland. New generations of squirrels and rabbits would stir in the oak groves and fence rows; frogs would once more peep and croak late into the night. And through all the passing seasons, the rising sun would cast its light on his father's grave, on his family's farm, on his place in the order of things.

Coming home was a time of reconciliation. He knew that he would not return with the innocence he had known as a boy. He was different; the old place was different. But, by returning, he had begun to understand the mystery of his own mortal relationship to the land. The place called home was a sacred place. Here, he could have faith in the world.

As a child,
Earl had been an intimate part of the landscape whose woods and fields
and sky measured the depth and breadth of his existence.
Standing on a hill, he would look toward the far ridges along the horizon
and know the immensity of the world.

The farm in the 1920s

Marjorie Quinney

Out West

Floyd Quinney

Seal Beach

Wedding, Floyd and Alice Quinney (center), 1930

Earl, May 16, 1935

Alice ("Ma") with Earl and Ralph

Floyd ("Dad") with Earl and Ralph

Ralph watering the Jerseys

School day

Merry-go-round, Dunham School

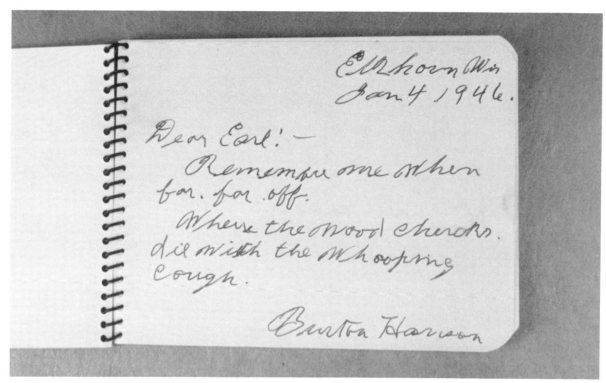

Autograph book

Corn knives and scythe

Hauling milk to Delavan

Earl on the Oliver 70, cultivating corn

Ralph mowing hay

Grain binder

Threshing oats, 1942

Fishing with Burton Hanson

Walworth County Fair

· *Mystery of the Marsh* ·

ON THE DAY OF his thirteenth birthday the boy feared that his life soon would end. All around him as he had grown up on the farm, he had seen life come into the world and vanish. Plants sprang from the earth each spring only to mature and wither with the coming of winter. He had watched the dying of farm animals, and he had grieved over the loss of his pet cats and dogs.

Now that his childhood was ending, the boy wondered what would happen next. Thinking one day that this would be his last year, he asked his mother to take his picture as a remembrance of his life. Standing on the milkhouse steps, squinting into the setting sun, he trembled with fear of what might come.

As the sun sank below the far horizon, the boy walked out of the long driveway lined with tall Chinese elms and down the winding road toward the old place. His ancestors had settled there nearly a hundred years before. On a gentle hill sloping to the marsh, they had built their house. They and their descendents had farmed the land.

But even before the settlers had arrived long ago, the land had hosted another people. A tribe of Potawatomi Indians had lived on the oak knoll that rose along the edge of the marsh. Among the trees they had built their circular houses of saplings, bark, and skins. They had fished in the creek that flowed through the marsh, and they had hunted in the surrounding woods. The boy's great-grandmother Bridget had told stories of seeing the Indians walking across the fields, looking at the place that had once been their home. Eventually the Indians returned no more to the marsh. He still looked for arrowheads in the plowed fields each spring.

Darkness spread over the lowland and moved up the hill. As the spring night unfolded, frogs at the edge of the pond began to croak. The shrill voice of a nighthawk fell sharply through the sky. A fox barked from the dark tamarack forest in the marsh. Numerous times the boy's father had warned him, "Don't go into the marsh." Clouds passed quickly over the full spring moon.

Finding a passageway under the crumbling foundation of the old house, the boy crawled through and rested in a corner of the cellar into the night.

·

As the early morning sun rose over the eastern hill and streamed through the cellar window, he opened his eyes slowly. Soon he became aware of someone standing in the doorway. A tall man with long hair braided and adorned with feathers and fur said, "I have come to look at the place that once was my home." The Potawatomi was dressed in buckskin breechcloth and leggings decorated with the porcupine quills and beads worn by a chief.

The boy was not afraid. He got up and came into the sunlight when the Indian beckoned. The Indian spoke again. "The ground upon which we stand is sacred ground. It is made of the dust of my ancestors." The tall Potawatomi walked quietly over to him and then said, "I have returned to teach you the ways of this sacred place."

The boy was about to be taken on a vision quest, a quest that Indian children before him had taken as they passed from childhood to the time one wore a full band of feathers. "I am ready," the boy said to the Indian.

They crawled through the passageway, and they walked together into the marsh. "The great mystery is all around us," the Indian said, speaking softly as they walked. "The birds that sing, the wind that blows through the trees, the earth upon which we walk, and the clouds in the sky are in sacred harmony." Looking out of the corner of his eye at the boy and in a sweeping gesture that seemed to encompass the horizon, the Potawatomi continued his teaching: "You must learn to look at everything twice. Look through the edge of what is visible and you will see the things that pass you in the dark. You must look twice if you wish to see fully the wonder of the world."

The boy squinted into the morning sun. "I am trying," he said. The light rays shot down sharply onto the surface of the narrow creek that flowed gently through the marsh. For the first time, he looked through the edge of the sun's rays and watched as the light danced on the water.

As he looked into the water and studied his reflection, the Indian spoke again. "You need certain experiences that will bring you face to face with what is true. One does not begin by learning something new, but starts by remembering what once was and continues to be. In order to know the marsh and all that is in it, you must experience the mystery of the place."

A ripple formed on the surface of the water, and then water splashed near the bank of the creek. Immediately the Indian said, "Watch carefully. You are about to see the creature of trickery and deception." Out of the water and up the soft muddy bank scurried a muskrat. Clutched in its front paw was some of the bottom soil that remained from the creation of the earth. Muskrat snickered and laughed slyly as he advanced toward them. "I am not what I seem, nor am I otherwise," Muskrat said clearly as he nudged the boy. The boy jumped back another step, tripping over the protruding root of an alder bush. "I am the furry creature that lives both on land and in the water. I come to confuse you, to show you that things are not always what they appear to be."

For a moment, all that the boy had learned to depend on as real during his childhood vanished. What had seemed fact now seemed to be a fantasy taking place before his eyes. Muskrat shook the water from his furry body into the boy's face. Was this an evil act or the natural behavior of an animal? The boy was confused, and he was frightened. He quickly slipped his hands into his pockets to keep them from trembling.

Muskrat did not stay long. He pushed hard with his hind legs and slipped into the creek. The boy looked around for the Potawatomi chief. With a happening such as this, he needed the guidance of the one who had come to him in the night. The Indian was right behind him, and he said to the boy, "You see, Muskrat goes away after you have entertained him."

Each day and night of the passing summer held an adventure. Several times, Muskrat reappeared, chuckling and then speaking another riddle. Muskrat continued his attempts to con-fuse the boy, suggesting the ambiguous nature of everything. Muskrat asked, "Can you hear clearly when you think about listening?"

This time the boy answered with his own question, "Can you think while you are speak-ing?" With this final encounter, Muskrat disap-peared into the creek.

The boy was learning to see the truth in the immediate and diverse things of this earth. He was learning to know the marsh as the Indian knew it. The meaning of life was found not in something far away, but in what was very close. The Indian said to him, "All that exists is in constant change and is always in the process of becoming something else."

And the boy, after a long silence, said, "I too am changing into something else."

The Indian loved the earth and all things of the earth. "Nature," he said, "is the whole of creation. To love nature is to love all that has been created by the Great Spirit."

In the late summer afternoon, the boy and the Indian rested together on the hill that sloped to the marsh, and they looked into the enormous white clouds that passed overhead.

•

The days of summer gradually changed their greens and blues into the golds and browns of autumn. The sun cast a warm glow over the marsh. Birds gathered in flocks and took flight. Spiders spun their intricate webs among the stalks of the drying sedge. Squirrels, scampering from their leafy nests in the oak trees, gathered acorns and nuts from the shagbark hickory. Two red-tailed hawks soared overhead on the flow of the wind.

In another time like this, the Potawatomi had celebrated the passing of the season. Gathering at the edge of the marsh, they gave gratitude for another year of abounding life. Men and women and children sang and chanted songs to the rhythmic beatings of drums. When a song was finished, a member of the tribe danced, and others joined in the dancing. Each person pre-sented a gift to another, a blanket, a piece of clothing, a bell, or a pipe. Smoke rose from the warming fire and curled high into the night.

The boy had other things to learn before the leaves left the branches of the trees. Walking deeper into the marsh, he and the Indian went into the tamarack forest. The Indian turned to him and said, "As you grow, you will feel a new stirring in your heart. It will come to you as a gift on the wings of beauty."

Suddenly, high on the dead branch of a tall tamarack, Great Blue Heron arched her wings. Ready to fly again a thousand miles into another marsh, she spread her six-foot wingspan and peered down at them. The Indian offered her a fish from the nearby stream. Great Blue Heron flew down close to the boy and the Indian and accepted it.

Her soft blue feathers brushed against the boy's legs. He reached out and stroked her long graceful neck. From her throat she whispered softly, calling as she did to those she loved. He felt a stirring in his heart, of what it might be like to love one as beautiful as Great Blue Heron. She whispered to him, "I will return to you another day." She raised herself, and throw-ing back her neck, opened her wings and flew into the sky. For a moment, the boy felt himself flying with her, suspended between heaven and earth.

He suddenly remembered his mother and father back on the farm. For an instant, he felt their affection pulling him back toward child-hood. A voice sounding like his mother's cried, "Please stay with me." The boy began to run, first in a direction that led to the farm, then in another that took him back into the tamaracks.

The late afternoon wind from the west was

blowing hard as they came out of the tamaracks. The harsh wind chilled the boy's face. Winter was coming. The boy and the Indian made a shelter together on the southern slope of the oak knoll.

•

The snow fell quietly, gently laying its soft white coat over the marsh. As the sun climbed above the hill to the east, black crows in the top of the hickory tree called *caw-caw-caw*. A winter mole burrowed deeper into the snow. Willows laced the lowland. High in the sky, wild geese honked in formation as they passed over the marsh. The boy and the Indian stepped down to the water's edge and washed their faces in the cool water. They then stood erect, facing the morning sun as it arched in the sky.

They left the shelter and explored the new winter day. "You are learning well," the guardian Indian told the boy. "Now I will show you where I have rested many winters." Walking up the hill among the oaks, they came to the mounds. The Indian said, "Long ago our graves were disturbed by those who were curious. Our bones, so carefully placed, were removed and scattered. Our spirits to this day wander restlessly over the land. We find some peace in the quiet of winter."

Bright stars shimmered in the stillness of the cold winter night. A full white moon cast a light on the hard surface of the icy snow. In the still night cattails stood silhouetted in the frozen marsh. Once the Indian spoke softly, saying, "Silence is the dry leaf that does not stir in the stormy wind. The mystery of the world is near to us when we are still." The boy was learning to keep his mind quiet and calm.

As morning neared, a dense hoary fog settled over the marsh. Shortly a wind began to blow out of the north. On the hill the frigid wind moved through a gully, long ago washed by the rains and melting snow. Pointing to the north,

the Indian called to the boy, "See, over the horizon, swirling in the wind is the Winter Witch. She moves in beauty but chills our bodies and our souls." In a lacy white gown covered with crystals of ice, Winter Witch circled the marsh and settled down on the other side of the gully. With her shining blue eyes, she stared at the boy, chilling him to the bone. He pulled his cap farther down on his head and zipped up his jacket.

Winter Witch spoke. "There are new lands to be won and souls to be taken." And then, her voice crackling like ice and thunder, she screeched, "I have come to take you." The boy felt her breath pass through him. A barren soul in lace and crystal, she stood very near to him. "I have conquered death in my own way," she said.

"You can have everlasting life, your own self forever, in your present form, if you come with me," said Winter Witch, her voice rising to the pitch of a scream. "You can be free of the ways of nature if you follow me. Winter can be yours forever." With these words, she reached for the boy's arm and pulled him away from the Indian.

The boy and the Winter Witch struggled throughout the gray dawning hours. Falling to the ground, they rolled down the snow-covered hill. When daylight came to the edge of the marsh, the boy lay locked in the icy arms of Winter Witch.

Signaling its place in nature, the sun began to rise over the eastern hill. And with the rising of the sun, winter's first warm breeze came out of the northwest sky. The boy slowly regained his strength, and with a strong thrust of his arms, he pulled himself free of Winter Witch. He shouted into the air, "I do not want to stay the same. I will not go with you." He ran to the side of the Indian. They watched as the crystalline gown of Winter Witch began to melt in the warm breeze that filled the marsh.

On the last cool current to pass through the

gully on the hill, Winter Witch vanished from the marsh. "A dead soul you must guard against all your life," the Indian said to the boy as Winter Witch rose into the few gray clouds that remained in the warming sky.

"The only everlasting self is the one that is in harmony with nature," the Indian told the boy. "The true self is always growing and changing, finally in death coming to be a part of all that is."

How strange this seemed to the boy the first time he heard it. He said to the Indian, "I will never be taken by the Winter Witch." The last snow of winter was melting on the hills and flowed gently into the marsh.

•

The warmth of new life spread over the land as the spring sun reached halfway into the sky. Over the far horizon to the south, Great Blue Heron appeared, her wings embracing the warm currents of the marsh air. Fresh and tender grass was turning the slopes green. In the woods the shooting stars raised their heads toward the sun. The mandrake plant spread its leaves over the early-forming fruit. On the hill north of the marsh the soft leaves of the mullein pushed through the earth. Perched on the new cattails in the marsh, red-winged blackbirds sang their songs.

In his journey with the Indian, the boy grew to love the marsh and all its creatures and living things. He learned that only through birth, growth, and death does life continue endlessly.

Change is necessary if we are to be a part of the mystery. In the years of travel that were to follow, what he had learned here would serve him well. "I feel at one with the mystery of the marsh," he said to the Indian. "The person I knew as myself when I first came to the marsh is no longer here. I am changing, and I am becoming a part of the wonder that is all around."

The last hours of the boy's adventure in the marsh were drawing to a close. He would be missed on the farm if he did not return soon. "My eyes are growing dim—I am old," the Indian said to the boy as they walked slowly toward the old place in the orchard. "I must leave you." When they reached the foundation of the old house, the Indian removed his soft moccasins and handed them to the boy. "These will be your walking shoes," he said. "They will take you far."

And then the Indian said, "I can return to my home now to rest in peace on the hill among the oaks with my people. We have come to know each other, and you have learned the mystery of the marsh. We can each go our own way now."

They embraced, and the boy went through the passageway. On the other side, the farm was in sight. With a pace more certain than when he had gone to the old place, the boy walked in his Potawatomi moccasins toward the farm, gazing with anticipation all the time at the unexplored horizon that spread out beyond. The western sky glowed brightly as he quickened his pace for the return home.

· *Leaving the Country* ·

WITH THE ENDING of high school and the beginning of college, Earl began his journey away from the farm. Eventually he would move away from the geographical region that is the Midwest, believing that travel into another world—out of the country—would create a new life. He had, in fact, rebelled against the Midwest. Why he was rebelling was not clear in his mind, but a change in his very being was the object of his longing. One January morning, after a heavy snowfall and a sharp drop in the temperature, the car would not start as Earl attempted to go back to college. His father attached the log chain to the front bumper and on the tractor pulled the old Plymouth until the motor turned. Pulling out of the driveway, Earl yelled back to his father, "I'm going to leave this God-forsaken land as soon as I can—and I'm not coming back!"

The first year away at college, Earl was assigned to a room in what was once an insane asylum. Constructed of yellow limestone quarried near Waukesha, the dilapidated dormitory was at the top of the long hill that sloped upward and away from the campus of Carroll College. He had selected the small, church-related institution, Wisconsin's oldest college, largely because it was not a favorite of the other students

at Delavan High School who were deciding to go to college. On trips to Waukesha with his father in earlier years, he had looked up the hill at the college from the implement shop where parts were being gathered for the Oliver tractor and the manure spreader. Once a student at the college, on the grayest winter days, he looked down the hill and remembered the times he and his father had taken trips to this place.

Several different students during the semester shared his second-floor room, but they quickly moved on to other possibilities. Earl was unaware of the worldly affairs amusingly enjoyed by his roommates. "Hey, Earl, who is Don Budge?" one athletically astute roommate had challenged. "A golfer, I guess," Earl replied. Earl finally asked for a room in another wing of the old building to escape the late-night parties and the smoke that was blown into his face as he tried to sleep. Most of all he missed being able to turn out the lights and go to bed early. He missed the bedroom at home and the calm bedtime voices of his father and mother.

The winter snow was piled high as he walked the mile down the hill to classes. It was cold and damp, and he was never dressed warmly enough. His head, with its close-cropped crew-cut, was always cold, unprotected by a cap. Boots were not worn even in the deepest of snow. Winter coats had little lining. In the years before the down parka, the wool cap, and pile-lined boots, students suffered in the cold and did not think it could be otherwise. The first year of courses in steam-heated rooms was a time of thawing out and returning to the cold again.

For the summer, Earl decided to continue with the job he had held the previous two summers, working in the National Tea grocery store in Delavan. The job provided him with his first employment outside the farm. It allowed him to be in town for whole days throughout the summer, and sometimes he stayed late for work on Friday nights. He enjoyed unpacking and stocking fresh vegetables and fruit, weighing them on the scales, and talking to customers. He caught the eyes of married women doing their daily shopping as he marked the bags of produce with a black crayon and placed the bags in their hands. He carried groceries to cars parked at the curb and placed them carefully in the back seat before saying good-bye.

One summer evening in June, following a day of work at the grocery store, Earl sat in a chair in front of the Colonial Hotel waiting for his mother to pick him up. The setting sun cast a golden light down the brick-paved street. Bold headlines on the evening paper announced the execution of Julius and Ethel Rosenberg. Still proclaiming their innocence of the charge of espionage, and after the final refusal of the judge to consider their appeals, they were turned into smoldering flesh in the electric chair. The *Milwaukee Journal* graphically detailed the final moments of their lives as the electric current passed through their bodies. Earl began to cry as he read about the Rosenbergs and what had been done to them that day. Senator Joseph McCarthy, dressed in a bombadier suit, had sent a postcard several years earlier to the farm, asking

his parents for a vote. The era of the witch hunt had followed. Now, through a newspaper report of an execution, Earl was becoming politically aware.

To escape the large and cold dormitory when he returned to college in the fall, Earl joined a fraternity located in its own house near the campus. On a moonless January night, with the temperature well below zero, the new initiates were blindfolded, abandoned on a country road far out of town, and told to find their way back. Earl was never able to accept the fraternal codes and refused to participate in the "hell week" initiation rites. He did his household duties, avoided the living room where players occupied the card table all night, and gave only minimal assistance in the ice-carving competition at the Winter Carnival.

Earl threw himself into his studies and other college activities. He had to prove his true worth to himself and to others. The pages of his grandfather's scrapbook contain some of the records of those years. Pictured in a clipping at the top of the page, Earl holds the gavel as the elected president of the student senate, the college's highest student government organization. In another clipping he is honored as one of the students selected by the student body for recognition in the 1955–56 edition of *Who's Who Among Students in Colleges and Universities*. Another clipping announces that he has been inducted into the national honorary biological fraternity—Beta, Beta, Beta—because of high scholarship in biology. He is also elected president of that organization, presiding over its annual autoclave dinner in the biology laboratory. Reported, too, are his participation in the annual Religion-in-Life Week and his chairing of the annual Mom and Dad's Day. In the scrapbook are the indications of the many ways Earl proved to the world his existence.

Without much conscious planning, Earl

took courses in sociology and biology. He continued to be pulled back and forth between these two subjects. His favorite course in his four years was one in field biology. Partly it was the biology of the natural world that attracted him, but it was also the chance to spend afternoons walking in the marshes around Waukesha, looking for aquatic plants and animals. To be out in nature exploring the edges of a pond, jumping from one bog to another, and walking over a hill and through a woods to another marsh helped to put his mind and spirit in a good place. Yet he felt that as a member of the human species he had a responsibility to all that was beyond the world of plants and animals.

The Methodist Student Movement played an important part in his undergraduate years. He was giving attention to a vague religious yearning. On lonely Sundays away from home there was a place to go where he could be with others. And there were car trips the students took together (always with the Reverend and Mrs. Blake) to visit other Methodist groups in Oshkosh, Shorewood, Appleton, and Superior in the far north.

In the spring the Methodist student group took the long trip to Lake Poinsett in South Dakota to a religious retreat with students from all over the Midwest. Once on U.S. Highway 14, the group traveled the width of Wisconsin and on through all of Minnesota. This was the farthest west Earl had ever been. Reaching the border of South Dakota, they passed through Brookings and then Arlington, near the homesteads of the brothers of his grandfather Quinney, and turning north they traveled the few miles to Lake Poinsett. By the second day of the retreat, Earl realized that he was not fulfilling the expectations of the occasion. Following the evening campfire meeting, as others were proclaiming that they had been saved, he felt nothing. Unmoved except for enjoying a beautiful spot on a pine-covered sandy beach at the side of a shal-

low lake, he returned with the group on the third day.

Only scattered memories remain of those college years, memories often attended by a vague melancholy and an occasional satisfaction that they can never happen again. Earl stands on the porch of Voorhees dormitory at one o'clock in the morning, ending a long courtship. He goes with fraternity brothers to hear Stan Kenton in Milwaukee. He plays Santa Claus in the Christmas program in an elementary school someplace near Brown Deer. He attends convocation on Thursday mornings in the gymnasium. He chips a front tooth playing a compulsory game of touch football. On the third floor of the gym he has to wrestle before going to chemistry class. He dresses in Hawaiian clothes for a sorority dance. In the spring he says good-bye to Julie, and they promise to go steady the next fall. She marries a senior during the summer and does not return.

Before the senior year began, Earl had to make a decision about his future occupation in life. With a major in biology, he could become a doctor. But was this the profession that called him? He had always been squeamish about the workings of the human body and the sickness that could befall it. He would put himself to the test and take a summer job in a hospital. So, in the summer of 1955, between his junior and senior years, Earl worked as an orderly in the surgical wing of Mercy Hospital.

He drove the twenty-five miles west to Janesville each day from the farm. Mother Superior at the Catholic hospital gave him lessons on authority and submission: "Always do what you are told, and never question the order of a doctor, even if you know you are right." The major responsibility of his job was to prepare patients who were scheduled for morning surgery. With a bowl of water and a razor, he would enter the patient's room, pull back the sheet, and shave the area of the body that was soon to be operated on. He then wheeled the patient down the hall and up to the door of the operating room, looking into the patient's eyes all the way and offering whatever comfort he could. He watched the operations—everything from simple D&Cs to surgery for major diseases like liver cancer. One morning he was handed a freshly amputated leg to be carried down to the lab for biopsy. He felt the dead weight in his hands. By the end of the summer, Earl had decided that he would not be a doctor.

As his senior year ended, Earl decided that he would attend the program in hospital administration at Northwestern University. At Carroll's graduation ceremonies, he stood in his black gown with his mother and father, his grandfather Will and Mabel, and his brother, Ralph, all squinting in the sunlight. On the way home, Earl told his family that he had not gotten a very good education at the college.

A few days after graduation, Earl drove with a former roommate to the East Coast, where the roommate was to begin graduate study in chemistry at Brown University. They looked at the sights along the way and spent two days in New York City. They drove up the Merritt Parkway and over to Cape Cod and then back to Providence for the night. In the morning, Earl began the return trip to Wisconsin, driving at a leisurely pace all the way home.

•

To gain some experience in hospital administration and to accumulate money for graduate work, Earl found a summer job at Chicago's Wesley Memorial Hospital. He drove from the farm to Chicago and moved into a large dormitory for Northwestern medical students. This was his first experience of living in the big city: eating in cafeterias along Michigan Avenue, walking the streets at night until bedtime, and going to the movies on Sunday afternoons.

He worked in the hospital's credit office

as an assistant to the manager, "Old Man" McCorkle. Earl's task was to call former patients and their families and tell them to pay their overdue bills. He spent the day at the telephone trying to collect money from people who could not pay. He was supposed to increase the threats with each repeated phone call. "You can't be too hard on them," McCorkle had told him. After the first few days on the job, Earl realized the cruel business that went on in the hospital, in an institution that he had thought to be humanitarian. And this was happening in a Methodist hospital.

Disillusionment with the hospital affected his plans for an education and career in the field of hospital administration. How could he be a hospital administrator if he had problems collecting bills? By midsummer the crisis in his career plans reached the breaking point. He called his former sociology professor at Carroll College, Dr. Tom Stine, and they arranged to meet at the professor's house in Waukesha. As it happened, Professor Stine's mentor had been Kimball Young, chairman of the sociology department at the Evanston campus of Northwestern. On an afternoon of the following week, Earl drove up Lake Shore Drive and Sheridan Road to the Evanston campus to meet Kimball Young in his apartment and to talk about changing to an academic career.

A large man, aging and by then nearing retirement, Kimball Young, the grandson of the Mormon leader Brigham Young, took Earl graciously and flamboyantly into the fold. Earl assisted Young in his popular undergraduate courses, expecting him at any moment to be swept away on a horse and taken into Utah country before the end of the lecture. Kimball Young referred to Earl as his "intellectual grandson" and autographed with kind words a copy of his book *Isn't One Wife Enough?*

Earl happily moved out of Chicago, forever relieved of administering a hospital and pleased with the thought of being able to be a scholar for the rest of his life. To pay for his room and board, he was assigned as a counselor and a keeper of order in an undergraduate men's dormitory. While receiving extra hourly wages by assisting Bill Bryon in his criminology classes, Earl learned about Bryon's adventures in getting Nathan Leopold released from the Illinois state prison. By the middle of the second semester, Earl selected a thesis topic: a study of the growth of the city and the increasing complexity, but not necessarily improvement, of human relations. In nine months, he had completed a master's degree in sociology.

•

He was already missing Wisconsin and the farm. On a Sunday afternoon in Evanston, after a visit from his parents, he became saddened to the point of tears. Making the break from home seemed to be taking longer than he had ever expected. The solution seemed to be to transfer to the University of Wisconsin. He made the necessary arrangements, and in the fall of 1957 he began his studies at Madison, having been granted an assistantship in rural sociology.

On his first Saturday night at the university, Earl went to the student union and wandered up to the ballroom where a dance was being held for new graduate students. The lights were turned low, the music played softly, and across the ballroom floor a woman headed straight in his direction. In nine months, this blonde southern woman in the blue angora sweater would be his wife. He pursued her relentlessly, and the following June they were married in the upper room of the Wesley Methodist Church. Every day that summer, Earl would run down Bascom hill from Agricultural Hall to meet Valerie in their apartment at the edge of Lake Mendota.

Back in his home state, Earl's interest in sociology began to turn to things more theoretical and philosophical. He was attracted to the

social theorist Howard P. Becker, who fascinated him with his intellectual breadth and his maverick character. Earl was moved by one who cared about ideas and who dared to pursue them.

An important part of graduate school was the association with other students. They gathered regularly in the local taverns along University Avenue or in the nearby bar known as Glenn and Ann's. On Friday nights Valerie and Earl would meet Jack and Ruth and Dan and others for a pitcher of beer and a night of country music played at the end of the tiny dance floor. Jack Rhoads was the most intense and inspired student Earl had ever known, and Earl learned much from him. Dan, the "Count" as Jack called him, had grown up in Czechoslovakia and had emigrated to the United States sometime after the Second World War. He had spent the war years on the run, supporting himself by collecting from alleys used prophylactics, which he washed, dried, powdered, and resold to the troops. Dan had secured enough money for his passage to the States by indicating to the United States Army the location of military bases on the borders. Pointing a stick to the large strategic map, he would please the officers each time he landed upon a site. Encouraged by their reaction and by the payment for each location observed, he had proceeded with the mapping enterprise for some time. Friday nights at Glenn and Ann's offered not only recreation for the week's end but also an education into another world.

Valerie continued to work on her own graduate studies in European history. Their apartment had a constant flow of graduate students in history, English, and the social sciences. As hardworking and often harassed married graduate students, they tried to accommodate to their separate work and common lives. Valerie became pregnant, and Laura Ellen was born that spring.

A new life began for all. With very little preparation as parents, Earl and Valerie managed day by day. Somehow they both continued graduate work and did basically the right things to assure the survival of the baby. On eight dollars a week, they bought groceries and baby food. With grocery cart and the week's laundry in the carriage with Laura, they carried out the weekly chores. Early on weekday mornings, Earl would put two eggs on to boil, hand Valerie the baby for nursing, and, after breakfast, hurry over the hill to the Quonset building to teach the early morning section of the course on marriage and the family.

In those graduate school days, students were encouraged to dabble in fields of study outside sociology. Earl took courses in the philosophy of science, physical and cultural anthropology, American history, social and intellectual history, and archaeology, as well as the full range of courses in sociology. He spent days of complete abandonment in a carrel in the university library and in the State Historical Society library. Gradually he began to focus on the relation of social institutions, especially religious and legal institutions, to the larger social and economic order. At a time in the 1950s when most graduate students were not exposed to Marxist ideas, it began to occur to him that the world was dominated by those with money and power. Gradually, in the context of the social activism of the 1960s, he would pursue these thoughts both in his work and in his life.

After three years, he tired of the student life and applied for an instructorship at St. Lawrence University. He took the flight to Canton, New York, for the interview. It was the first time he had been in an airplane, except for the time his cousin Dean had landed in the hay field and taken each of the Quinneys on a flight over the farm. In a week he received the offer and accepted a job that would begin in the fall. Then, early on a June morning, Howard Becker, Earl's mentor, suffered a brain hemorrhage and died. Both out of mourning for Becker and out of

anxiety for his own uncertain future, Earl took to the basement for several weeks and built a four-drawer desk that would serve him for years to come. Marshall Clinard, who was returning to Wisconsin after several years of research on crime in India, agreed to be Earl's new adviser and dissertation director.

To pay the rent for their apartment while they were in graduate school, Earl and Valerie managed the old Victorian house in which they lived on Murray Street. Owned by the university, it contained four apartments on the first two floors and some rooms—usually vacant, it seemed— on the third floor. The major part of their job consisted of maintaining the coal furnace in the basement during the winter months. The responsibility kept Earl busy running home between classes several times a day to shovel coal to fuel the furnace and to remove huge, red-glowing clinkers the size and shape of automobile tires.

On a Saturday night in August, an explosion rocked the whole house and brought out the fire department to extinguish the fire and take bleeding bodies down the stairway. After a night of investigation, a university official explained that a gang of Milwaukee teenagers had been using the apartment next door to the Quinneys on Saturday nights. And on the night of the explosion, someone lying on a mattress on the floor had flicked cigarette ashes into a Coke bottle that held gunpowder used to shoot pigeons on the roof. (That explained why Earl had noticed small bird bones in the garbage cans that he took regularly to the street.) Earl and Valerie also learned that rooms in the house had been used on weekends for prostitution. After learning about the shady happenings that had been occurring around them, and feeling lucky to have survived the explosion, Earl and Valerie decided that the time was right for leaving Madison.

They packed the Renault—a car that never should have been bought on graduate student finances—and drove down to the farm for two days. Then they headed east to that part of New York called the North Country. Earl drove steadily and without much relief. They stopped only a few times along the way for comfort. Laura spoke her first complete sentence: "I am hungry."

•

Another midwesterner was now wandering away from home, thinking that he must leave the homeland in order to leave home. Much of the rest of his life would be the search for a home in another part of the world—beyond the homeland.

Perhaps the leaving was to be a part of the returning. Certainly the leaving furnished him with a growing perspective and finally a search for the meaning of his life. John T. Flanagan, another commentator on the leave-taking of midwesterners, especially among those who would become writers, observed that "the Midwest spawned them, educated them, gave them a theme and a framework in which to express the theme, provided them characters and events, and in the long run, determined their message and its expression." Possibly a distancing was necessary before the return.

Years later, when he thought more about returning than leaving, Earl read the poetry of Edgar Lee Masters. In *Spoon River Anthology*, Masters wrote an epitaph for another midwesterner who observed his own life when it had passed. The poem ends with the lines:

> To put meaning in one's life may end in madness,
> But life without meaning is the torture
> Of restlessness and vague desire—
> It is a boat longing for the sea and yet afraid.

Earl feared a life without meaning, a life of being forgotten on the farm. With all the longing in the world, he hurried down the road. It was in a direction away from what had always been home.

· *On the Road* ·

FOR TWENTY-FIVE YEARS, I traveled away from home. Near the end of that time, I began to wonder about the meaning of this journey called life. Walking the streets and byways of Providence, Rhode Island, with church steeples and smokestacks on the horizon, I started to ask questions that had been missing from my life as I had traveled from one place to another. The words of Roger Williams, upon entering this place centuries earlier, inspired me: "And having in a sense of God's merciful providence unto me in my distress called the place Providence." I read the religious writings of Paul Tillich and learned that "faith in divine Providence is the faith that nothing can prevent us from fulfilling the ultimate meaning of existence." I closed my own book *Providence* with a benediction: "Let us begin again to hear the word, to see the vision granted unto us."

Sensing a prophetic possibility in each moment, but not knowing how to use the image drawn in the Judeo-Christian tradition, I turned to the mystery of the unknown. The opening verse of the *Tao, Te Ching* would finally inform my journey toward home:

> Before heaven and earth
> There was something nebulous
> silent isolated
> unchanging and alone
> eternal
> the Mother of All Things
> I do not know its name
> I call it Tao.

My home ultimately would have to be found in all the mystery of the universe.

In Providence I began the search for the way back home. I thought about the person who had left home and who would become the one I now know as myself. The road I have traveled has taken me to places north, south, east, and eventually west near the homeplace. Reveries of those years on the road helped bring me home again. I daydreamed as I searched for a meaning in my life. The past came back to me as moments in the present.

•

I was coming into a strange new world as I drove from Wisconsin to Canton, New York, at the end of the summer of 1960. The world that I was entering required a learning and a development in new and different realms. Is one ever prepared for the journey? Does growing up in one place and time prepare one for what is to follow? I was about to begin my first adult job in a field I hoped to advance. With a wife and child, with the beginning of demands that would continue to impinge upon my life, with a political world rapidly changing about me, with all these things I traveled into the decade of the 1960s.

The Korean war had ended, and the battle casualties had been heavy. The United States was waging a Cold War against the Soviet Union and Red China, led by President Eisenhower's secretary of state, John Foster Dulles. There was news of military aid being given to South Vietnam, and of a communist-led guerrilla movement in Laos. Mohammed Mossadegh of Iran had been overthrown in a coup organized by the Central Intelligence Agency (CIA) and was replaced by Shah Rezi Pahleve. The Suez Canal had been nationalized by Gemal Abdul Nasser of Egypt. Leading a revolution in Cuba, Fidel Castro had overthrown Fulgencio Batista. In May 1960 Nikita Khrushchev announced the shooting down of an American U-2 spy plane over the Soviet Union. Washington promptly replied that the American plane had strayed off course on a meterological flight.

We arrive in Canton and settle into the first-floor apartment of the university-owned house located directly across from the campus. We sleep on the living room floor until we can buy a mattress. I begin teaching the four courses I have been assigned for the semester. We feel lost, far from home, and in the wrong place. The farm country around Canton is beautiful in the fall, although many of the farms and small villages are economically depressed. We drive into the Adirondacks and up to the St. Lawrence River and then into Canada. Laura, in the back seat, rides in a crib.

Winter weather comes early to the North Country. Soon each day is filled with quietly and continually falling snow. The Thanksgiving turkey carcass will not become unfrozen from the bottom of the garbage can until late in the

spring. People who die here during the winter months are stored in the garage of the funeral home until graves can be dug. I am preoccupied with a heavy load of teaching and with worry about dissertation research that I must design and complete.

We begin to make friends. Becoming aware of the world around us, we talk about current events. We discuss the ramifications of the Cold War policy of the United States, military spending, and the threat of nuclear war. We closely follow the 1960 presidential campaign. On a neighbor's television set we watch the debates between John F. Kennedy and Richard Nixon. Kennedy wins the debates and the election, and Eisenhower delivers a farewell address to Congress about the military-industrial complex. The arms race is on Kennedy's mind as he gives his inaugural address: "Let every nation know, whether it wishes us well or ill, that we shall pay any price, bear any burden, meet any hardship, support any friend, oppose any foe, in order to assure the survival and the success of liberty." He ends his speech with a plea for negotiation, but as we watch, a peaceful time does not seem to lie ahead.

The New Frontier promises to solve everything. The Peace Corps is formed to take American skills and goodwill to the Third World, assisting countries to develop along American lines. The Alliance for Progress is designed to advance economic development in Latin America, attempting at the same time to avert revolutions that would go against American interests. In spite of criticism that more money should be spent on human needs, Kennedy is committed to "landing a man on the moon" before the end of the decade. In February 1962, John Glenn becomes the first American astronaut to orbit in space. He follows by a year the orbiting of the Russian's first man into space, Yuri Gagarin. The space war is to continue.

In the spring of 1961, about twelve hundred

Cubans who have been trained and equipped by the CIA in Guatemala land on the southern coast of Cuba. The invasion at the Bay of Pigs is successfully pushed back by Castro and his troops. At about the same time, Vice President Lyndon Johnson visits South Vietnam, and a force of Green Berets is sent to help train the South Vietnamese army. Back in Cuba, the Soviet Union is helping the Castro government to build missile bases to protect Cuba from another American invasion. Kennedy declares that the missiles must be removed. During a few days in the fall of 1962, in their exchanges and negotiations, Kennedy and Khrushchev come close to starting a nuclear war.

While all this is going on, I complete a dissertation on the criminal behavior of professionals. I have traveled to Washington to obtain records and have conducted interviews in Albany. I defend the dissertation successfully in Madison, and late in the afternoon Valerie, Laura, and I go to a downtown theater to see the movie version of *The Music Man*.

At the end of two years, the dean of the faculty at St. Lawrence approaches me and angrily asks, "Why are you leaving this university?" I reply, "I have given you and the university two good years of my life." It is time to move to another place.

•

We make our way south in the small, blue-green Renault. Coming into Lexington, Kentucky, on the Winchester Pike late in the evening, we stop for the night at a motel with a brightly lit courtyard. The next day, as we move into the little house near the campus, the head of the University of Kentucky's sociology department brings a casserole to our door.

Thousands of acres of Kentucky bluegrass fields with white wooden fences trailing over hills are spread out behind stately country mansions. In town, out of sight of middle-class

houses, along the railroad tracks, and behind the tobacco mills and warehouses are the unpainted and dilapidated houses of blacks. During much of the year, the sweet odor of curing tobacco hangs over the city. On a bright November afternoon, I walk downtown after teaching a sociology class. Along the way, the pace of the traffic begins to change. Radios are reporting the first eyewitness accounts of a shooting in Dallas. Later it is confirmed that Kennedy has been assassinated, with shots apparently coming from the book-depository building in Dealy Plaza. Lyndon Johnson is sworn in as the new president as Kennedy's body is flown across the country to Washington. A few days later, we watch on live television the shooting of the assassination suspect, Lee Harvey Oswald, as he is being transferred from the local jail.

During the three years in Kentucky, the summer of 1962 to the summer of 1965, we become involved in the civil rights movement. The demand for civil rights for blacks is being felt throughout the United States, but the antagonisms and contradictions of segregation are especially evident in the border state. Cyrus Johnson, a friend in the sociology department and a North Carolina native, is an example to me of the role whites can play in the civil rights movement.

In 1962 the University of Mississippi is desegregated when a black student, James Meredith, accompanied by federal troops, walks through the doors of the university. This action is followed by demonstrations of marchers in Birmingham, Alabama. Soon Governor George Wallace is forced to desegregate the University of Alabama. In August 1963 Martin Luther King, Jr., leads the march on Washington. In front of the Lincoln Memorial, King speaks eloquently of his dream of an America where racial equality will someday be realized. A quarter of a million people sing "We Shall Overcome," the old Baptist hymn that has become the marching song of the civil rights movement. Back in Lexington, we are demonstrating on the steps of the federal building and marching to the state capital in Frankfort in protest against racial segregation.

My thoughts in sociology are being shaped by what is going on around me and by my participation in daily events. Why, I ask, does the law make some behaviors criminal and others legal? My main development in criminology during this period is learning to see crime as a political phenomenon. Future consideration of crime clearly must be within a framework that places it in the struggle for control of the social order.

In the meantime, as travelers in another place again, we make new friends. We are brought into a circle of friends in the English department. We discuss new developments in literary criticism and popular culture. We attend the university drama productions, dance at the local night spots, listen to jazz and bluegrass music, and sip mint juleps at Derby time in May. In the dazzling sunlight beside the swimming pool at the university's playground for the faculty, I read for the first time Albert Camus' *The Myth of Sisyphus*. I too am having the existential feeling of rolling a heavy rock up a hill and having it roll down again. But I share Camus' joy: "The struggle itself toward the heights is enough to fill a man's heart. One must imagine Sisyphus happy."

In the basement of our rented house, I construct a study where I work late into the night beside the warm furnace. Valerie continues to work on her dissertation in French history. Laura plays with other children in the back yards and parks within a few blocks of the house. I begin to think of myself by a different name. I am told by a friend that my middle name, Richard, suits me much better than Earl. On identification cards, social security forms, and other legal documents I change my first name to Richard.

What am I to be called by my mother and father, brother, and relatives back in Wisconsin? I am in a new world far away from my origins.

With increasing commitment to leftist politics, I make arrangements to bring Norman Thomas, the several-times socialist candidate for president of the United States, to the university to speak. Securing funds from the sociology department, several graduate students and I write to Thomas in New York and propose a visit to Lexington. He agrees, and a few weeks later we meet him at the airport and chaperon his visit. Although Thomas is getting old, he delivers his lecture with the vitality of a much younger man. Arriving for a dinner on his behalf, he eases out of the car with his fur cap folded in hand and is assisted by the restaurant attendant. Thomas says, responding to the offer of help, "I can make it; I'm just getting old." The attendant then tells him, "You will live to be as old as Methuselah." Thomas replies, "I feel that old now." The following day we drive Norman Thomas to his next speech in Richmond, Kentucky.

At a meeting of sociologists, I am introduced to the chairman of the sociology department at New York University. The following year, the NYU sociology department is looking for another sociologist to be hired at the rank of associate professor. I am contacted and fly to New York for an interview. In New York City, we lunch in a step-down restaurant on the north side of Washington Square Park in Greenwich Village, and the dean, who is an English literature scholar, is impressed that I am currently reading *Tristam Shandy*. After being in the big city, the center of the world it seems, I know that I will take the job if it is offered.

•

We leave Lexington in the middle of the summer of 1965. Laura is crying as she waves good-bye from the back window of the car to her friends. Valerie and I have not given ourselves the chance to have second thoughts about leaving. A day later, the spectacular skyline of New York City appears early in the morning as we drive down the Palisades Interstate Parkway. Passing over the George Washington Bridge and moving with the heavy traffic on the West Side Highway, we exit onto Twenty-third Street and make our way down to the Village. We find an apartment on the second floor of the Washington Square Village housing complex. After three days of receiving parking tickets because of confusing alternate-side-of-the-street parking regulations, Laura and I drive the rusting Renault over the Brooklyn Bridge and sell it at a junkyard for ten dollars. We will not need a car in New York City.

Henry James had lived nearby, on Waverly Place. Edward Hooper and his wife had lived in their studio in one of the row houses on the north side of Washington Square. John Reed had also lived on Washington Square. E. E. Cummings once lived and wrote in a house on Patchen Place. Still existing bars and saloons have been the meeting place for literary figures. Dylan Thomas had frequented the White Horse Tavern. Eugene O'Neill had staged his plays in the theater on MacDougal Street. And now Cafe Chino is presenting the latest in avant-garde theater. I stroll around the fountain in the middle of Washington Square Park on Sunday afternoons listening to folk singers. Rhythm groups are harmonizing under the arch. I begin to take a serious interest in photography. I take extension courses at NYU with Sandra Weiner and spend days circling Manhattan, learning to photograph.

Running against Barry Goldwater, Lyndon Johnson has been elected president, Hubert Humphrey vice president. The Great Society proposed by Johnson is supposed to be dealing with the nation's problems of poverty, discrimination, ignorance, and urban decay. Meanwhile, the United States has stepped up its involvement in Southeast Asia. Congress has passed

the Tonkin Gulf Resolution, empowering the president "to repel any armed attack against the forces of the United States and to prevent further aggression." The resolution, in effect, has become the legal basis for full-scale American involvement in Vietnam. By the end of 1965, the war has escalated, and close to two hundred thousand American troops are in Vietnam. A local civil war on the other side of the world has become Americanized.

By the end of 1967, nearly half a million American troops are in Vietnam. They have dropped almost three million tons of bombs on the small country. Large numbers of civilians have been napalmed and killed, and much of the land has been turned into a wasteland by chemical defoliation. Yet the Vietcong has not been "pacified," and the infiltration of troops from North Vietnam has not halted. American casualties are high, and the war is beginning to strain the United States economy. A war costing twenty-five billion dollars each year is forcing cutbacks in Great Society programs. Then, in January 1968, the Tet offensive is launched by the Vietcong, bringing heavy casualties to both sides and destruction to many cities and villages. An American officer explains after the total destruction of a village, "It became necessary to destroy the town in order to save it."

Opposition to the war gradually increases. In New York City, there are marches down Fifth Avenue. In October 1967, we ride to Washington on a bus to the huge antiwar demonstration. Led by Norman Mailer and Robert Lowell, we march over the Arlington Memorial Bridge and up to the steps of the Pentagon.

At the university, students and faculty begin to question not only the war but also the role of the university in the United States. We ask, "Whom does the university serve?" We want a change in the university and demand that students and faculty have a role in governing the university. Curriculum and grading changes

I argue in my writings and in professional forums that our academic work is—and must be—political and that our work should provide an understanding that allows us to make the necessary changes in the social and economic order. What a good society might look like, beyond the liberal notions of equality, civility, and humane social relations, is yet to emerge. Right now, there is the need to develop a critical analysis of the existing social order in the United States.

Manhattan Bridge

Under the Brooklyn Bridge

Battery Park

Staten Island Ferry

West Fifty-seventh Street

Boccie, East Houston Street

Delancy Street

Bellevue Mental Hospital

East 102nd Street

The East Village

Day of Moratorium, Washington Square Park

Second Avenue at St. Mark's Place

At the General Motors Building, Ecology Day

East Fourth Street

Central Park

War tax resistance at the Internal Revenue Service

The East Village

The Boardwalk at Coney Island

Coney Island

Coney Island Beach

Washington Square Park

are suggested, and we alter our own classroom methods. At one point, in reaction to continuing resistance by the university administration, I, along with two other faculty members, decide to form a pact to give all students a grade of A. Sidney Hook of the NYU philosophy department attempts to have the faculty senate censure us. Our actions are based on the assumption that in changing the trappings of higher education, the foreign and domestic policies of the United States will change. Only later would we develop a better understanding of the nature of the United States.

Out in Washington Square and over in the East Village, along First and Second Avenues and over in Tompkins Square Park, another form of resistance is taking place. "Hippies" and "flower children," as they are called by the media, are on the streets and in the lofts. There is a new counterculture of be-ins, love-ins, marijuana smoking, LSD trips, electronic music, rock festivals, and new styles of dress. The revolution seems to have arrived. Abbie Hoffman comes to talk in my class. *Hair* opens at the Public Theater on Astor Place.

Meanwhile, a revolt is taking place among urban blacks. Faced with problems of unemployment, inferior education, and poor housing, they begin to demand improvements in social and economic conditions. Moving beyond the call for the abolition of legal and political barriers to civil rights, blacks want jobs and living conditions equal to those of whites. A black nationalist mood is strengthened by the 1965 riots in Watts, California. In 1966, the National Guard puts down riots in Chicago, to be followed by the 1967 riots in black neighborhoods of Atlanta, Tampa, Cincinnati, Newark, and Detroit. Blacks are becoming radicalized, symbolized in the call for black power. The Presidential Commission on Civil Disorders somberly concludes that "our nation is moving toward two societies, one black, one white—separate

but unequal." Shortly afterward, Martin Luther King, Jr., is assassinated in Memphis. On television, we watch the funeral and the day of mourning around the nation.

Believing that my work in sociology and criminology has to be part of what is going on, I argue in my writings and in professional forums that our academic work is—and must be—political and that our work should provide an understanding that allows us to make the necessary changes in the social and economic order. What a good society might look like, beyond the liberal notions of equality, civility, and humane social relations, is yet to emerge. Right now, there is the need to develop a critical analysis of the existing social order in the United States.

What is needed at this time is a reorientation to the study of crime, a theoretical perspective by which research in criminology can be reinterpreted and current happenings can be understood. My work in criminology takes on new meaning and purpose. I argue that when we examine crime as a human construct, in a politically organized society, we are able to raise new questions about justice. I conclude the preface to *The Social Reality of Crime* by writing, "I contend that a relevant criminology can be attained only when we allow our personal values to provide a vision for the study of crime."

Although some members of the NYU sociology department, as in other departments throughout the country, try to carry out a policy of "business as usual," others, like me, argue that these are not usual times and that academics are never removed from the world. Divisions develop within the sociology department, with alliances shifting as members continue to become radicalized during the various events and debates. I am promoted to full professor, but this seems fairly inconsequential in these times. I feel that I am fortunate to be in the midst of political ferment.

In our Washington Square apartment, we live

like New Yorkers. We attend off-off Broadway plays, shop for groceries at the Grand Union, walk Eighth Street and browse in the bookstores, see the latest foreign films, attend lectures and poetry readings, go to concerts at Lincoln Center, and meet friends in bars along Bleecker Street. I often go uptown during the day to museums and department stores. Laura attends P.S. 41 on Twelfth Street near Sixth Avenue, plays between the apartment buildings, and goes with her friends to Washington Square Park. On Christmas Eve, we sing under the Washington Square arch with other Villagers. On New Year's Day, we take a taxi to the Upper West Side for a festive gathering with friends.

As the 1968 presidential election nears, our interest returns to electoral politics as a way of resisting the war in Southeast Asia. Senator Eugene McCarthy announces that he will seek the Democratic presidential nomination. His candidacy is a rallying point for the peace movement. We form the Washington Square Neighbors for Peace, working for McCarthy and raising money for antiwar demonstrations. President Johnson, finally exhausted by resistance to his Vietnam policies, announces that he will not run for reelection. He promises steps toward a deescalation of the war, and peace negotiations begin in Paris. A final cease-fire in Southeast Asia is not to come until January 1973, after an invasion into Cambodia by American troops and months more of antiwar activity.

Robert Kennedy enters the Democratic primaries against McCarthy. The night of his primary victory in California, after his victory announcement, Kennedy is shot and killed. At the Democratic National Convention in Chicago, in the midst of Mayor Richard Daley's repression of demonstrators, old-line delegates nominate Hubert Humphrey to be the presidential candidate. This is followed by Richard Nixon's Republican candidacy. In the fall election, Nixon defeats Humphrey by a considerable majority.

We are involved in many things as the 1960s draw to an end and the 1970s begin. In the summer of 1969, Valerie, Laura, and I go to Yugoslavia to see what socialism really looks like. We spend the following summer in Madison. My mother, who is trying to learn to live without my father, visits us. One morning in the middle of the summer we are awakened by an enormous explosion before dawn. The Mathematics Research Center at the University of Wisconsin campus has been torn by a bomb set in reaction to the Vietnam war. The explosion occurs in the same building in which, ten years earlier as a graduate student, I learned sociology.

Valerie is pregnant throughout our summer in Wisconsin. We had decided that it was finally time for another child after waiting all these years since Laura's birth. In the fall, on November 14, Anne Holloway is born, one year to the exact date since the death of my father. Laura welcomes Valerie and the baby home with a bird-of-paradise flower as we return from the hospital.

It is time for my sabbatical leave from the university. I am tired of being a professor, and I have been teaching for ten years without relief. I have become a full professor in a major university, and I am asking, Is this what I want from now on? There must be something else. I feel out of touch with the natural world.

Living in New York is becoming too much a life of consumption, not only of material goods but of culture as well. All around are the constant stimuli of commerce and culture, which I find a growing burden. I write an essay with the title "From Repression to Liberation," in which I suggest a need for a transcendental mode of knowing, a critical stance that allows us to oppose the existing order and prompts us to move into a new age. I write: "This means that we cannot continually share in the comforts of the known and the established. We must be willing to push our lives to unknown limits."

•

We ready ourselves for the road again. Rather than sublet the apartment in New York so that we can be certain of a place to live if we return, we give it up and move out completely. In our minds, we are entertaining the possibility of never coming back to New York. By evening, the twenty-foot U-Haul truck has been loaded. Laura and I are in the cab of the truck. Valerie and Anne will wait until morning for the airplane flight to North Carolina. Derek Phillips, my colleague at NYU, shakes my hand good-bye, and with the truck already pulling away, he shouts, "Have a good life." Laura and I head into the Holland Tunnel and are soon on the New Jersey Turnpike, headed south.

Chapel Hill, North Carolina, is a place that promises to offer what we need for the year after living for six years in New York: a small town, a chance to live closer to nature, a warm winter, and a university with an excellent library. Yet we know few people here, so it is another place where we will have to start over. I am beginning to realize that I do not take easily to change, but my life in Chapel Hill is to be a time for change, and changes for which I am not very well prepared.

My own personal and political values are in transition. In my academic work I am moving beyond libertarian values and constructionist theories of social reality. I suggest that only with the collapse of capitalist society and the creation of a new society, based on socialist principles, will there be a solution to social problems. I start working on several book manuscripts that will eventually be completed and published.

My notebook is filled with ideas and proposals for directions that I might take next. There are outlines for several books, including a proposal for a book on growing up in Wisconsin. There are notes on how I am reacting to my idealist philosophical position of the past, that I

need to consider more seriously the materialist basis of social reality. My purpose continues to be to expose the realities by which we live and then to propose alternative realities. I must have a sense of what could be, as well as an understanding of what is.

I begin to make a series of trips to other universities. I am asked to speak about the changes that are taking place in my work. I am in demand because I seem to represent what is happening to some academics, and what is happening in the social sciences as a result of the changes over the last decade. In Lexington, Kentucky, I give a lecture and meet with graduate students in sociology, and I am excited about the enthusiastic response I receive.

In April 1972, I fly to the University of Montana in Missoula. I lecture to faculty and students in a program on law and crime sponsored by the National Institute of Mental Health. I enjoy talking about new ideas and telling people about my unorthodox intellectual and political views. I am beginning to think of myself as the circuit rider coming to bring the new message. In Missoula I become aware of the contradictions warring within me: transcendence versus involvement in the immediate world; security versus change; family versus solitude versus communal living; knowing versus uncertainty. As on a quest, I fly from Montana to Berkeley, California, a center of the Free Speech Movement in the 1960s, a place where student radicals protest and organize against the war, and the location for counterculture changes of various kinds. In the criminology school at the University of California, faculty and students have been leaders of a West Coast radical criminology. I spend most of my time in Berkeley with these people, at parties and in long talks about everything from crisis politics to communal living, from music to Marxism. After a week, I fly back to Chapel Hill.

Within a few days, I am off to the University of Minnesota for a two-day symposium on the sociology of deviance. Before flying back to Chapel Hill, I stop at the farm to see my mother and to celebrate my thirty-eighth birthday. The following week I am in New York to chair the Ph.D. dissertation defense of one of my NYU graduate students. I note that during the year I have moved from some sort of anarchism to phenomenology to an underground Marxism. I am told that I have not lost my "style." Back home in Chapel Hill, I drive to Asheville with my botanist friend Lytton Musselman, who also is from Wisconsin, for two days of botanical watching and hiking.

The first part of the summer of 1972, we stay in Chapel Hill. I have decided not to return to my job in New York for the next year, taking another year's leave and avoiding a final decision about moving back to New York. Royalties from my several books will provide just enough money for us to live on during the year. We have bought and moved into a house on Tinkerbell Road, a house with a balcony across the front and woods in back. The campaign for the 1972 presidential election is proceeding. We are enthusiastically working for George McGovern. Then, early on the morning of June 17, five men with cameras and electronic surveillance devices are arrested after breaking into the Democratic National Committee Headquarters located in the Watergate apartment complex in Washington. It is discovered that the leader of the break-in is connected with the committee to reelect Richard Nixon. The Watergate affair begins with the cover-up and continues through the trial of the five burglars, the Senate hearings, and the final resignation of Nixon, a course of events that will take place over the next two years. We decide to spend the rest of the summer in Berkeley.

On returning to Chapel Hill, I become immersed in the local community. There are friends in town who have come out of the southern populist tradition, and there are people who have remained from the counterculture days. We start to talk about creating a socialist community. I bicycle to the university library daily for several hours of research and writing in my faculty study. Laura attends a Quaker high school in the country. Valerie and I alternate afternoons of child care when Anne returns from nursery school.

From September 1972 to May 1973, I continue to make trips to give lectures at various universities. I am invited to Sangamon State University in Illinois to present a series of lectures on the American State. While in the Midwest, I fly to Wisconsin to see my mother and visit with Uncle Lloyd and Aunt Elsie, who are getting very old. My mother and I drive up to Ripon to see Ralph and his family. I note that I am still bothered during these visits by the isolation in the country.

In March, I am invited to a debate at the University of North Carolina at Charlotte on "The Future of American Society." In April, I fly to Indiana University in Bloomington to participate in a symposium on new approaches to law and crime. At the end of the month, I fly to Tallahassee to give a lecture at Florida State University. With one of my former graduate students, I drive to see the Gulf of Mexico.

I have decided not to return to my tenured professorship at New York University. I am doing things in Chapel Hill that are not possible in New York while holding a full-time teaching job. I am helping to write and distribute a socialist monthly newsletter that we call *Bread and Roses*. I write a critique for the newsletter about the city-manager form of government. Following the publication of the article, the mayor appoints me to Chapel Hill's Charter Revision Commission. Tony Thomas, an anthropologist friend who teaches at the university, and I teach a free, nonuniversity course on Socialism and Everyday Life. There is a "one-man" exhibit of my photographs at the gallery of the Wesley Foundation.

Southern country-rock music is being played in the local bars. Throughout the summer of 1973, the Watergate hearings are shown on television. I make one more trip to Berkeley.

I sense that one period of my life is coming to an end. I have lived with the idea that these are extraordinary times, that actions beyond the ordinary are necessary if we are to move to a better society. I am trying to be a force for change in the existing society. When the roll is called, I want it to be noted that I have been doing the right things on earth at a crucial time in history.

The divergent forces within me have to be reconciled. Between the end of October and the summer of the following year, I go through what can only be regarded as a crisis. It has been coming for some time, an accumulation of much that has happened and much that has been un-attended to since my middle twenties. I had left New York and a university professorship to find something that was being stifled by that way of life. Chapel Hill seemed to be a new beginning. There were few structures to be locked into; all was in flux. I could write outside the bounds of academic sociology; I could make friends on the basis of myself rather than my role as university professor; I could try to practice socialist relations in the community; I could have a garden and play on the lawn with my children; I could walk in the woods again. In some ways, all these things have been realized, but in all of this there has been the making of other problems, problems that were not anticipated. Without the structure of a full-time job and other supporting networks and interests, I am without an established order for living my life.

Once again, at the end of August 1974, it is time to move. Valerie has gotten a job as an assistant professor at the University of Rhode Island. We will live in Providence. I will have a visiting professorship at Brooklyn College and the Graduate School of the City University of New York, commuting between Providence and New York. We load the U-Haul and begin our drive north on the interstate highways. Laura and I are in the cab of the truck, and Valerie and Anne are following in the blue Dodge Dart. We have sublet the house in Chapel Hill and have rented an apartment in Providence. We are uncertain whether we will ever return to Chapel Hill. The possibility of starting over is appealing.

•

Traveling through an unfamiliar world, filled with both threatening and sustaining forces, I wonder if there is to be any triumph in the journey. On my mind as I travel once again is whether this experience will take me home. My time in Providence will become filled with the search for the meaning of my life, the search for the meaning of human existence. Instead of being like a ship battered by a stormy sea, I am looking for something that will help chart my course.

After a difficult first year of adjusting to a new place and a new life, we establish a frame-work for living in Providence. I occasionally teach courses, depending on our economic needs, at Boston University and Boston College. I secure an adjunct professorship at Brown University, which provides a faculty study in the library, a study high on a hill, overlooking Providence. Although I have chosen to be on the fringes of academia, I continue to maintain my professional activities in sociology, as associate editor of several journals and as a participant in the annual meetings of professional organizations. I continue to make trips across the country to give lectures at various universities. My photographs are shown in galleries in Providence. Essentially I live on the fringes of academia so that I will have the time and energy to be a full-time scholar.

I am creating a world, and Providence is

the stage from which all else is viewed. I walk the streets downtown. I hike along the Seekonk River and stroll to Wayland Square. I walk shaded paths past eighteenth- and nineteenth-century houses, and always I am in the place. An interior monologue, a stream of consciousness, flows in my head. I am like Leopold Bloom of Joyce's *Ulysses*, imagining a world in the course of the day.

It is becoming clear to me that my years of writing have been shaping my life and that the solitary act of writing is creating a certain form of life. One cannot spend day after day of writing alone without having the process affect the manner in which one conducts oneself in the rest of the world. I am developing a style that requires ever more solitude and time for reflection and writing. I am becoming what I am writing.

I identify myself with a Providence writer of a former time, H. P. Lovecraft. Within a hundred feet of the library study where I work each day is the site where Lovecraft lived the last years of his life. Writing horror and fantasy tales by day, he would venture out at night along the hilly streets of Providence. His life was devoted to his art and to his image of reality. The magic of his writing was discovered by other generations after his death. His gravestone in the Swan Point Cemetery proclaims, "I am Providence." In devotion to a place, Lovecraft lived his life.

Writing has for some time been my principal means of communication—with myself, with others, and with the world. I write to create a reality for myself, to clarify my thoughts to others, and to make contact with a world that seems inaccessible to me in other ways. Writing is, existentially and theologically, a way of being in the world. In writing I am trying to give meaning to the world and to my life.

As I prepare for the writing of *Providence*, I make what strikes me as a breakthrough in my thinking. I start to see that the historical materialism of orthodox Marxism is a product of a thought that emphasizes material conditions to the exclusion of transcendent and religious values. Marx had an image of an essence beyond current existence, but the essence was primarily secular, another material existence. Paul Tillich and other theologians, in contrast, pointed to the importance of our essential nature, which is spiritual. We do not live by bread alone. To be human is to create a world that allows for our spiritual being as well as our material existence. What kinds of conditions hinder or promote the realization of our spiritual selves? The problem is one of combining the material and the spiritual. Through the window of Providence, I consider the problem.

I am now on a pilgrimage, drawn by the desire for satisfactions not supplied by the world as currently known. After twenty-five years of excluding religious questions from my life, I am returning to questions that are necessarily religious. The religious element that was missing from both my work and life now is to be renewed. Using the language of the Judeo-Christian tradition, I begin to speak of a prophetic voice in the world, of a union with the eternal. Walking the city of church spires that reach into the sky, I sense an atmosphere filled with the daily presence of the divine.

Becoming ever more important to me is the search for a meaning that would give guidance to a whole life. At this time, after completing my travels through Providence, I recognize that we humans, myself in particular, need a purpose, one that is ultimate and that bears on eternity. Addressing the question of purpose in my writing, I return to the traditional metaphysics of our Western culture, the Judeo-Christian image of God. But after completing that project, I begin to wonder whether, as some theologians had been arguing for some time, we might be reaching the end of the Christian era. Perhaps we are nearing an age when another image of our essential being is needed.

My thoughts during 1979 are directed to this question of meaning. I assume that it is a question that is crucial to everyone. A critical problem of our contemporary culture is that the question of meaning is not given more attention. Perhaps we have not yet created the symbols that are appropriate for our age. In other words, I am looking for a purpose and a place, a home in the world. Realizing that the crisis in contemporary society is as much theological and spiritual as it is economic and political, I proceed with metaphysical reflection. The central symbol of God, especially, must be reconstructed so that spiritual concerns will be significant for contemporary life. The project, it appears to me, is to reconstruct the central metaphysical notions by which we live and have our being.

Deeply embedded in our historical consciousness in the metaphysics of traditional Christianity and in the epistemology of the social sciences is the division between the sacred and the secular. The world, accordingly, is divided into two separate realms, the secularity of "this world" and the sacredness of the "other world." A vastly different way of thinking about the sacred and the secular is to recognize the sacred quality of everyday life. All human experience is of transcendent importance within this world. When we attend to the transcendent meaning of the universe in our everyday lives, I suggest, we begin to find a home in the world.

•

On a Sunday afternoon in January 1980, I board an airplane for the flight from Providence to Milwaukee. For several months, we have been debating whether I should accept an offer of a full-time, tenured teaching position at the University of Wisconsin at Milwaukee. The job, requiring another move, certainly would ease our financial situation. I would be returning to the place that physically seems to be my home. A full moon glistens on newly fallen snow as I land at the Milwaukee airport.

I stay in Milwaukee only for a semester. We will not make the move. I miss the familiar land-scape of Providence that I have grown attached to over the last six years. Milwaukee's physical landscape does not appeal to me. It hurts me that Anne is having a hard time accepting the move. In fact, the child in both of us is rebelling against another move. I write her a story that begins, "Many days and nights ago, far, far away in a place much like our own lived two friends by the name of Urple and Little Whitford," to be played on a tape recorder whenever she misses me while I am gone. Landing at Boston's Logan Airport, I ride the Bonanza bus south to Providence. As I enter Providence, I have the feeling that Lovecraft must have had years earlier when he returned from an absence of several months. I had read the passage from Lovecraft's story to friends in Providence several times before. Lovecraft, after months of longing for his home, in the person of Charles Dexter Ward, makes his way up the hill toward home. "And at last the little white overtaken farmhouse on the right, on the left the classic Adam porch and stately bayed facade of the great brick house where he was born. It was twilight, and Charles Dexter Ward had come home."

I think that I am fortunate to be able to return to Providence, to the place where I have lived the longest since leaving Wisconsin twenty years earlier. The rest of my life can be spent here, where I have developed a form of life that seems to fit me. Soon, however, the feeling begins to fade. Something has happened to me in the attempt to return to Wisconsin. I am losing my hold on Providence. Something new has been set in motion as a result of my return to Wisconsin. Life will never be the same for me in Providence.

We have to move from our house on University Avenue. Anticipating the move to Milwaukee, we had sold the house. Friends help us move from the old house to another a few blocks east, on Holly Street. Once moved, I begin to hear sounds I never heard before. The noises of Providence, even louder in the night, bother me. Factories on the Seekonk, the power plant of Narragansett Electric, air conditioners on houses, traffic on I-95, children next door, all make a noise that hurts my ears and disturbs me throughout the summer. I miss the old neighborhood.

At summer's end, after presenting two papers at the annual meetings of the American Sociological Association in New York, I decide not to write for a while for an audience of professional social scientists. What I have been writing in sociology is too far removed from what is currently happening in the field. Instead, I will work on ideas that relate to my own life struggle. I am impressed by Montaigne's observation: We carry within ourselves the whole form of the human condition. In my notebook, I record that I am attempting to bring *nature* into life, that nature is a symbol and reality that gives meaning to our lives. I make a note to myself: "The primary creation is nature, and we are a part of that nature." Our human interventions in the world are divine or demonic depending on whether or not they are in harmony with nature and the universe.

For the next year, nature is to be my text. I am the explorer looking for the hidden meaning of the everyday wonders of the natural world. In nature I am now looking for a home. I hope to make the discovery before it is too late. I read the lines of A. E. Housman: "Here, on the level sand / Between the sea and land / What shall I build or write / Against the fall of night?" The spiritual journey is toward enlightenment. I listen to the natural flow of things in the wholeness of the universe.

I have the feeling that I am being reabsorbed into that from which everything springs. I am being nurtured by the wonder of the natural world. With awe, I walk the hills and woods of Providence. I am preparing for that time when I, as a part of nature, will be returned to the land and to the water and to the air. The realization is as sobering as it is liberating. Our human part

in nature is revealed in the lines of the Swedish poet Pär Lagerkvist:

Some day you will be one of those who lived
    long ago.
The earth will remember you, just as it remembers
    the grass
    and the forests, the rotting leaves.
Just as the soil remembers,
    and just as the mountains remember the winds.
Your peace shall be as unending as that of
    the sea.

Faith in nature, I write, signifies our coming home, our finding a place in the world. It is a discovery of what was there all the time. We search for human community and for a oneness with the world. To come to the revelation that we are part of the natural world—that we have a place in the scheme of things—is to find that we are at home in the world. With the homecoming that is ours through nature, we recognize our place in the human community.

I will continue to be close to the world of nature. Yet I still ask whether a place for my habitation can be found. Can there be a home that is more than in the self? When will we be in a time where there is a greater home than the self? The world of nature allows us to dwell beyond ourselves. But I still long for a concrete physical place in the world that I can call home. I have written about the search for a transcendent meaning, I have written about the nature of the world, and now I am asking about the place called home. As always, for me, thinking and writing are ways of being in the world, ways of seeking the meaning of the world.

I finally make the note to myself: "I am a midwestern American writer, a regional writer from Wisconsin." My life has been that of one who grew up in the Midwest, journeyed from it, and now seeks a return. I have come from a particular place in a former time to my life as a witness in our time. My search for home is a search leading to a loss of myself in a communion with the world beyond the self. On the midwestern farm, I am part of the land. In the midwestern landscape is a mystery that I have felt in my life since my earliest childhood. I long to return.

I have become aware of the changes I have undergone since coming to Providence, changes in the body that are in the schedule of aging. In a few short years my eyes have changed so that I can no longer read the print of a book or a newspaper without removing my glasses and holding the material very close to my eyes. I have become nearly an inch shorter. A tailor making an alteration in my old coat tells me that my right arm has lowered and my left hip has risen, both a result, he says, of carrying a briefcase habitually in my right hand. I am sensitive to noise, and a high-pitched ringing in my head comes and goes.

I make notes while visiting friends on Schoodic Lake in Maine: That which I experience as melancholy is a combination of processes, forming in varying ways at different times. My form of life, a life as observer, writer, and philosopher, has isolated me. Looking into the universe has produced an *ontological* melancholy, a realization that the meaning of the universe cannot be comprehended. I, like all of us, am a wanderer in the cosmos, a wanderer searching for a meaning that ultimately eludes us. There is also the *psychological* melancholy that comes from the way I have chosen to live: without secure employment, with movement from one place to another, and with long periods of solitude. Yet my melancholy, which I learned early in my years on the farm in Wisconsin, is part of the process of becoming human. I have been going from one life stage to another, promoted, enhanced, and exacerbated by the questions that I have asked about life's meaning. The ways I have met and resolved experiences in the past have served me at later times. I still desire to be where the secret things can be entertained.

And I wonder: What price has been paid? For a long time, I have been living my life for my art and believing that the production of ideas is important for the world and that I am making my contribution to the world by writing about the world as it is and as it could be. I am now without money, a secure job, and a permanent home. My form of life has not provided for some of the things that could serve me and my family. What has been the worth of a lifetime that is now beyond its halfway mark? How can a life be put together?

I am tired of being a wanderer. It is time to return home. There is only one place that I feel at home: in Wisconsin, on the farm. But a short time ago, when given the possibility of moving near it, I did not stay. What is going on? There is a mystery here that is very close to home. I will stay near the question. As Rainer Maria Rilke advised those who seek: "Be patient toward all that is unresolved in your heart. Try to love the questions themselves." I have been living with the questions for some time.

We return home to find our place in the world, a place in which to lose ourselves to the world. The return home provides us with a dwelling place for the continuation of our life. In the place we call home, we put down roots, and we love others and the world; it is there that we become truly human. The farm in Wisconsin furnishes me with an image of what is home, the deeply loved visible place that draws me back and, finally, allows me to be on the journey home.

Preparations are being made. I awake from a dream. My father has been planting trees up the driveway to the farm. He has planted them for my return. In the spring of 1983, a letter comes to our house from a university in the Midwest, from Northern Illinois University, generously offering me a job. In the summer, we move back to the Midwest. The search for home will continue in the homeland. From now on, it will be a different kind of journey.

*Traveling through an unfamiliar world,
filled with both threatening and sustaining forces, I wonder if there is to
be any triumph in the journey. On my mind as I travel once again is
whether this experience will take me home. My time in Providence will
become filled with the search for the meaning of my life, the search for
the meaning of human existence. Instead of being like a ship battered by
a stormy sea, I am looking for something that will help
chart my course.*

Basement on the farm, November 1969

The granary

In the attic of the farmhouse

Back alley in Elkhorn, Wisconsin

On the way to Ripon, Wisconsin, Country Trunk D

Haven Motel on Highway 12, Fort Atkinson, Wisconsin

Photographing in New Glarus, Wisconsin

Laura, early morning, passing through New Jersey on the train from Greensboro, North Carolina, to New York, April 1970

Carrboro, North Carolina

Bedroom, Chapel Hill, North Carolina, spring 1974

Third-floor stairway, Providence, Rhode Island

Atwells Avenue on Federal Hill, Providence

Sachuest Point, Rhode Island

Anne, Hundred Acre Cove, Rhode Island, October 1977

Schoodic Lake in Maine, August 1981

Between the farm and DeKalb, late fall 1983

· *Lodging for the Night* ·

GREAT-GRANDMOTHER BRIDGET, sitting in the kitchen chair placed beside the lilac bush, watched the movement along the far ridge to the south. Two Indian men, two squaws, and a boy walked toward the oak knoll in the marsh. They had returned once more to say farewell to the place that had been their home. Bridget told my father of the sighting along the ridge, and he in turn told me. Growing up on the farm, I thought about the Indians who had lived on the oak knoll. From the beginning, I wondered if I belonged on this land. In search of my own place, I have been a wanderer all my life.

After forty years of travel, I walked along the ridge and found my way through the marsh and climbed up the hill to the tall oaks on the knoll. I, too, had returned once more to the place that had been my home. This time I carried with me my daughter's pet, which had died a day earlier. I would bury the dead pet in the sacred ground among the Indian mounds. A red-tailed hawk soared overhead, watching me with my burden as I prepared the burial place. I muttered something about returning the animal to the elements of all creation. A strong fall wind blew over the hill from the west. I shivered from the mystery of the act I was performing as much as from the chill of the wind against my face. I remembered

the Indians who had been forced to leave their land, and I feared for my own uprootedness even as I stood on the land of my own beginnings. I hurried out of the oaks, retreating through the marsh and up the ridge to the road, just as dusk descended over the gray day.

A story is told among Orientalists of the pious rabbi of Cracow who traveled far to find a treasure that in a dream lay buried under a distant bridge. Finding the bridge, he was told by the captain of the guard that in his dream the treasure was to be found, not under the bridge, but in Cracow, in the house of the rabbi. Returning home, the rabbi discovered the treasure in a neglected corner of his house. The treasure had been very near all the time. But it could be discovered only in a journey to a distant region and in an encounter with a stranger.

I, too, had traveled far in search of the treasure—for the meaning of my life—and I, too, had returned. Yet my story had not ended with a certain discovery of the treasure. It still eluded me, the treasure of feeling at home in the world. Could it be that the treasure is not literally in the place, but is buried deep inside me? Another journey of even more uncertain territory lies ahead. If the treasure cannot be found, I am doomed to be a wanderer all my life.

Bridget and her husband John fled from Ireland during the potato famine of the 1840s. On my mother's side of the family, the Holloway brothers left North Devon when they no longer could survive on Lord Fortescue's estate. "Come to America," a relative wrote to one of the brothers. "You will be able to make a home here." I am removed from their travel and settlement by only a few years of time. I grew up on the edges of their frontier; I am a product of their movement over the land. And by the fact of my chosen profession, I am an itinerant moving across the modern landscape.

Were they ever at home, the Potawatomi who lived on the oak knoll, Bridget and John who settled on the land, and my father and mother who made their life on the place? Did they feel a oneness with the world, a peace that comes with being at home? Or is this a question that only we moderns ask of our lives? We move from one place to another looking for the treasure. Each house we inhabit in the journey holds the promise of a treasure. Yet, in the end, I suspect, the treasure of being at home in the world will be found inside ourselves. The ultimate journey is to a far place that is very near.

•

"All that we are is a result of what we have thought." I did not know the words of the Buddha when I was young, but I have lived a life formed as much by thought as by anything else. True, wandering from place to place has been a requirement of my profession. Like the poor scholar in an Irish folktale, I have visited the homes of many along the way. But did I not, out of my early thought, choose to be a wanderer on an uncertain journey? And did I not continue the journey with the thought that I had to move geographically in order to nurture the soul? Thought has made a life.

Two images, which are seemingly at odds, have commanded my attention since the snows

began to fall this winter. They have come from a time long ago. On a road that winds through the ice-age bluffs of southern Wisconsin, I ride with my father and mother and brother to the farming town of Whitewater. Along the way we pass the house of a man who lives the solitary life of a hermit. Through the small window of the tar-papered shack, I see the hermit sitting in front of a kerosene lamp as we pass in the winter's night. In the summer, he is seen only occasionally, working the crop that he has planted beside his house. He is one of the old ones who live alone and who are not understood by those who pass on the highway. The hermit has lived his whole life in this one place.

Around the bend from the hermit's house, we pass the deep pond that fills a kettle in the moraine. In the center of the pond, a figure protrudes from the surface of the water. It is the head of a wooden horse. I have waited with great anticipation to see the head of the horse rise from the water another time. Each time we pass by, I am in awe of the horse in the pond. We are molded by the mysteries that enter our lives.

The head of the horse, emerging from the water, seems to be in such contrast to the hermit, so firmly settled. Only with the passing of many years did I learn that the early Greeks had their own myth about what I was experiencing as a farm boy on a trip through the bluffs. The myth is of Bellerophon, forced to leave his native land soon after growing to manhood. In a misunderstanding with the King of Argos, he has to move from one country to another. Fleeing across the sea to Lycia, Bellerophon is ordered by the king of that land to find and destroy the Chimera, the invincible monster that lives in rocky caves and ravages all the country around. Bellerophon, even with all his courage, needs help in the task, and Minerva tells him to ride the snow white, winged horse, Pegasus. On the mighty Pegasus, Bellerophon springs into the air and flies like a shooting star through the clouds to the country where the Chimera lives. He slays the monster and says good-bye to the noble and divine winged horse.

Pegasus then rises into the sky and speeds away like lightning. The winged horse is never mounted again by any mortal being. Some say that Jupiter set the winged horse among the stars. As for Bellerophon, a later telling says that because of his eager ambition and the success that led him to think "thoughts too great for man," the gods became angry. The mortal rider of Pegasus wandered alone, devouring his own soul and avoiding the paths of others until he died.

The hermit may never have seen the pond and the flying horse that emerged from the water around the bend in the road. The hermit had his own thoughts. As in the solitude of Henry David Thoreau in a cabin at the edge of Walden Pond, the hermit knew the importance of being in one place. The hermit had no need to fly into the sky on the winged horse Pegasus; possibly he had the imagination that had its own wings, making physical flight unnecessary.

Thoreau writes in his chapter on solitude, "While I enjoy the friendship of the seasons I trust that nothing can make life a burden to me." He then asks the rhetorical question, "What do we want to dwell near to?" The woods are full of companions. "Shall I not have intelligence with the earth? Am I not partly leaves and vegetable mould myself?"

The hermit may have said to himself what Thoreau tells us: "I love to be alone. I never found the companion that was so companionable as solitude." In a paragraph Thoreau gives us the secret of the solitary mind. It is what is surely known today as Zen mind: the mind that is at home with itself because it is aware of its relatedness to everything else. Thoreau tells us from his cabin in the woods, "By a conscious effort of the mind we can stand aloof from actions and

their consequences; and all things, good and bad, go by us like a torrent." "I only know myself as a human entity," he writes, "the scene, so to speak, of thoughts and affections; and am sensible of a certain doubleness by which I can stand as remote from myself as from another." Each life is, as Thoreau concludes, "a work of the imagination."

The winged horse and the hermit's life are two different ways to gain access to what is beyond the ego-centered self. Imagination allows us to fly outward into a sky where mysteries of the universe dwell. The hermit takes a far journey inward. The hermit, a secular version of the desert fathers of the fourth century, made known to us by Thomas Merton, is lost "in the inner, hidden reality of a self that is transcendent, mysterious, half-known, and lost in Christ." Both the winged horse and the hermit are released from the prison of a confining selfhood; both are on a journey that takes them into the larger world, to a union with the otherness of existence.

We moderns are on our own journey of transcendence. We may seldom speak of coming closer to God, but our journey is the same no matter how we talk. And for many of us today, the journey inward is also a journey across the land. We think that we must move from one place to another to find the meaning of our lives. Will we ever come to a resting place that we can call home?

I look back over my shoulder at the ridge where the Indians returned each season. I, too, continue to come back to the place, to the place of my birth. I long for a sign, an answer perhaps to a question that remains unclear. It has something to do with a oneness with all creation, perhaps a form that can come only with death. Maybe I am preparing. As I hurry up the hill, I remind myself again of Rilke's advice to those who seek: "Be patient toward all that is unresolved in your heart. Try to love the questions themselves." And the image of the mortal Bellerophon on the great winged horse Pegasus cautions me to be careful in the questions I ask. Live closely to the reality of what is here and now in this place where there is all the wonder of the world.

Rather than be among the scientists, I prefer to dwell with the alchemists, among Loren Eiseley's wizards "who loved the living world, loved mystery, kept talking birds close to their shoulders, never solved a thing but lived close to where solutions were and did not want them, preferred mystery." The leafless shoots of the lilac bush stand quietly along the foundation of the old house.

•

The slim crescent of the new moon rises over the southern ridge. The dark night has come quickly. Leaving the place once again, I drive down the road and out to the main highway, which will take me south through small towns and across low-lying prairies. Signs at the crossroads name the roads of farm families that have stayed on the land for generations: Crowley, Streit, Lembcke, Dunham, Melms, Collins. Half an hour ago, I had left the country road named Quinney.

A fog begins to form, rising from the fields, and moves gently over the highway. Yard lights on the sides of barns casting bluish lights cut through the gray fog. I slow nearly to a stop when an occasional car approaches from the opposite direction. The lights of roadside taverns brighten the way along the sparsely settled farmland. On the edge of a town, near the state line, the orange neon sign of a dealer beams OK Used Cars.

I near the town that I currently call home. Turning onto Somonauk Road, a trail once walked by the Indians who lived here, I make my way hesitantly along the few remaining miles. At home, my younger daughter, an ado-

lescent now, does not ask me the question about what happens to animals when they die. The mystery of life—without answers—has entered her world.

Only a short time ago, I had walked daily the streets and byways of another place. Roger Williams, the pious seeker, had inspired the naming of the city out of his own condition: "And having in a sense of God's merciful providence unto me in my distress called the place Providence." I, too, searched with all my occupation for the meaning of a life, and I tried to find the source of the melancholy that cast its long shadow over my days.

It would seem that after all the years of thought and intellectual endeavors, I would have gained an understanding of my life and its meaning. But I had reached a point where something more than thought and knowledge were required. Days and nights—turning into years— I had wandered around Providence. Gradually I began to sense a spirit of a former time that hovered over the steeples of the eighteenth-century New England churches. Questions not raised in modern science began to emerge. The streets of the city led to a place of the spirit that I had not traveled before. The heart quickened as large white clouds formed in the morning sky over the bay and moved in over the city.

What is the purpose of this long seeking but a preparation of the soul? In searching for a place, I have desired to return to the source, to be complete. The fifteenth-century Hindu and Sufi poet Kabir asked, "Do you believe there is some place that will make the soul less thirsty?" I was beginning to find, as I walked the streets in quiet meditation, that home must be found wherever I am, that there is no place where one cannot find wholeness.

The years have passed, and I have left the city; but I cannot say that I have finally found a home. I think that I know the way to travel if a completeness is ever to be found. I no longer ask with such frequency, "What is the meaning of life?" I try to avoid the mortal rider's tempting of the gods with questions that are too great. The meaning is very near at hand, in the mystery of this place where I am now. Yet how am I to live in peace and harmony with the meaning that is there all the time? In this small midwestern town, where I moved to be near where the Indians once lived, I look out along the horizon and know the difficulty of practicing what is so simple.

The delusion that we are separate from all other things in the universe is hard to break. Perhaps, most likely, the delusion of separateness serves a civilization that has lost the old way of being an integral part of nature. To be in harmony with the world and all its creatures is not a vision shared by economies and political systems that depend on dominance and conflict for their existence. The American Indian who declared, "The earth and myself are of one mind," and the Eastern sages, who for centuries have shown the compassionate oneness with others, offer a new way that is a very old way. It is so simple a way that we moderns find it difficult in our hearts and minds to accept. We suffer each day in the modern delusion of the self isolated from the rest of the world.

We easily become attached to what does not exist. This sorrow that I feel comes from the memory I hold of the dead things of yesterday. Krishnamurti tells us, "It is yesterday that is sorrow and without cleansing the mind of yesterday there will always be sorrow." Thought itself is sorrow; it is a melancholy of the soul. In a meditative living of each day, I am trying to be aware of the thought that fills the heart with sorrow—and I am trying to let it go. The modern mind is always restless, chattering like a monkey moving from one thing to another, one place to another, and desperately remembering what has been. I walk among the willows, counting the leaves, and I try to free the mind of the words

and memories that imprison me. In emptiness there is a closeness to all that is. There is great beauty beyond all thought and emotion.

A quieting of the mind can come in the awareness of the impermanence of all things, and in ceasing to insist that it is otherwise. A Buddhist master of the Rinzai sect in fourteenth-century Japan warned, "Always bear in mind that life, whose gravest problems are birth and death, is impermanent." Likewise, because there is no entity that can be known and experienced as a permanent self, the desolate image of isolated and unrelated beings is dispelled. A contemporary Buddhist, Stephen Batchelor, tells us, "As this new vision unfolds, our basic anxiety and our sense of meaninglessness are dissolved in the growing awareness of the profound mystery of interrelatedness that permeates all phenomena." I trust that as I begin to arrive at this original home of my relationship to all of nature, I will know who I am, and the treasure may be found.

This morning I begin again, reminiscing about the past and, as I have done for years, fantasizing about the future. I am removing myself from the present moment, as if thinking will aid me in transcending myself. This, I realize, is not truly the way to transcend the self. But old habits, grounded in the ways of the West, do not die easily. The past and future are simple thoughts in the present. "All that we are is the result of what we have thought," *The Dhammapada* again reminds me. The sorrow of the present moment is the memory of a past that no longer exists and a future that will never be when it is the present. Time is thought; and the thought of time is sadness. There is only one question left, and the asking of the question is the answer. The asking is what is happening now and in this place.

My writing at this moment is an unfolding of my own emptiness. I am experiencing the impermanence of all things. A Zen master in Providence ends his evening Dharma talk with the parting words, "I hope you only go straight— don't know, get Enlightenment, and save all beings from suffering." In awe, in awareness of this moment, I am at home. The rays of the morning sun bounce against the oval mirror as the red squirrel jumps from limb to limb.

•

What is our life every day but a spiritual journey to an unknown land? We keep returning to the places of a former time and then moving to new places in our search for a home in the world. In the shelter of a house we seek a place where we can be in peace, where we can experience a place in relation to all other places.

Wizards in this age, we live close to the solutions but do not find them. It may be that we prefer mystery to the answer. More likely, though, we who dwell on this vast land cannot fully live the solutions even when knowing them. With a restless mind that desires more to know than to be, a mind that clings and judges, a mind that fears the void, we will not quiet ourselves. In the sadness of thought, we crave what does not exist. The poor wandering scholar finds shelter only in the home of others.

Still another time I make the trip back to the old place. The wooden horse in the pond, existing now only in my memory, no longer rises from the water in the moraine. Nothing remains of the hermit's shack at the bend of the road. The Potawatomi left long ago. Even their chief, Shabbona, told them, "The red man must leave the land of his youth and find a home in the far west." The wild animals are here no more, having gone toward the setting sun. The lush pastures of the farm are now tangled shrubs and matted grasses.

The problem is that of finding a basis for our lives in the midst of turmoil and suffering. Dogen, thirteenth-century founder of the Japanese Soto sect, wrote a text that is appropriate for our time: "In life there is nothing more than life, in death nothing more than death: we are being born and dying at every moment." Everything, even that which we call the self, is constantly changing from moment to moment. We arrive at the original home when we become aware of the flow of our existence. Beyond that, we accept the mystery, and we are compassionate.

The ridge merges into the horizon. I sit quietly, like Thoreau, being "sensible of a certain doubleness," watching thoughts as they rise and fall and move on to something else. The clouds pass above, and there is little memory of them as new clouds appear in the western sky. The honking of geese overhead, the call of a jay, the breeze rustling dry leaves in the oak tree, all these break down the memories that haunt the restless mind. The wonder of the universe is in this place, and eternity is in this moment. But the mind remembers the passing of time. Walking away again, the poor scholar needs lodging for the night.

· *A Traveler of Country Roads* ·

ANOTHER COUNTRY SONG, "On the Road Again," comes over the car radio: "On the road again—goin' places I've never been—seein' things that I may never see again." The road this time stretches out of town over the prairie and through the farm country of northern Illinois. I have decided to spend the summer alone traveling the roads of DeKalb County. As with all travel, no matter how near or far from home, every moment is a journey of the soul. We spend our lives traveling.

It is time for me to travel across the prairie that surrounds the place I now call home. I am ready once again to be on the road, on a multitude of roads that will lead only to the edges of the county. Travel of such proportion already seems to be of eternal consequence.

In a white car as if on a great steed, I set out from town at noon each day that is graced by a bright sun. The roads follow the grid pattern of the Midwest land, and I go north, south, east, and west. The stated purpose of my deliberation is to photograph the rural landscape. I have received a small grant from the university that will justify my travel along the roads. I will document the changes that are taking place in this rich agricultural county, a movement from small farms to large farms, the transformations brought about by agribusiness. Still I will see a landscape that is timeless. The transcendent quality of the Midwest, one that survives all human constructions, has to do with the line of the horizon, the way the sky meets the land, the drift of clouds over the fields, the way the sun reflects against the weathered barn. This is the landscape that has brought me back to the Midwest after years of travel in another place.

I watch the sun rise high in the sky. White cumulus clouds float over the prairie as I drive out of town. This is a good day to be photographing. What I am looking for is not yet clear. A discovery of some kind, a way of making some sense of this wandering journey. I put on dark sunglasses and turn on the radio to WSQR, "Northern Illinois' Country Connection," from downtown Sycamore. The land before me is already taking on a heightened look. I place the K2 yellow filter on my 35-mm camera. Merle Haggard sings his current country song, "Someday When Things Are Good I'm Goin' to Leave You." This is the country I left years ago and have returned to at this moment in my life. Maybe I will be able to see anew. There is always the possibility of a rebirth, of an awakening.

Of late I have taken to looking at what is

very near in any search for the ultimate. Whether I believe in God is no longer the pressing issue. How could I, how could we, ever know enough to believe in God? Belief is not the issue. How to live daily with a faith in a meaningful existence is the contemporary concern. We are seekers in a world where traditional answers are no longer convincing. We are travelers who aspire to reach beyond the material rationalism of the modern age. The sights and sounds along the country road have a double meaning. They suggest that we are indeed in the world but not of it. Through the camera's view finder all things have a second look. I see the world with a slant.

I turn onto one of the many dirt roads in the county. "Travelin' with the rodeo is the only life I know. . . ." A large, yellow dog dashes from the farmyard. "You're the toughest cowboy in town. . . ." Holding the wheel with one hand, I grab the camera and shoot the dog in motion. "I've always been a travelin' cowboy—now there's no place left to go." The dog gives up the chase. I wish I had tried to settle down. Why this longing of the heart?

The dark blue, cloud-filled sky rises above the great expanse of prairie land. The space beyond the town changes the sensibility of the mind and spirit. At first, one becomes lost in the immensity of the surrounding country. But soon the vastness becomes part of oneself. I, the beholder of the open country, now measure the depth of my own nature. I have become part of the landscape, another creature of nature among many others that share the land, air, and water. In a reshaped space I am, as Gaston Bachelard suggests, elsewhere dreaming in a world that is immense, both outside and inside. I travel through the country to enter a new realm, to change my nature and to become the nature that I am. This is the landscape of my birth and of my daydreaming when young. I am now in a land near home. As the cultural geographers

have reminded us, there is something close to essence, to truth and beauty, in the land of our birth. The land holds a mystery we seek to grasp. The traveler is a gnostic, an artist and a theologian, delving into the mysteries held by the particular place. We travel in this land to know its secrets, and in so knowing we become part of the landscape.

From the fields, the sweet smell of clover in blossom flows through the open windows of the car. On this late June afternoon, red-winged blackbirds perch on the fence in the lowland. The white clusters of Queen Anne's lace sway along the roadside in the warm breeze. The telephone poles stretch to the end of the road. I turn left to put the sun at my back and watch the shadows fall against the buildings of another homestead. Merle Haggard's words play softly from the radio: "I'll be one more man that you can say you've had. . . . Someday soon I'll be just one more memory." Now a strong odor enters the car, and I know I am near a pigyard.

For the land to become a place of mystery, we must first imagine the actuality of the place. Without imagination, a poetic imagination, the natural and built environment is without interest, subtlety, or mystery. Only with imaginative effort does the landscape become humanly real. Thus attuned, we are encouraged to dream, to imagine the places of the body and soul to which we may yet journey.

On the road, we are engaged in imaginative play. This thing we call self is immersed in the present moment of travel. The conscious self is lost in a self that is larger than itself. Children in elemental play, we drop our conventional adult selves and become intimately bound to an unhindered space. Each moment of unlimited time is now without beginning or end; we are in eternity. We are choicelessly unfolding, undifferentiated from all else, in a land with which we are ultimately one.

The camera becomes the mind's eye as I travel in the country. With camera in hand, I see what otherwise remains hidden. Mysteries are revealed when I am ready to look, and the presence of the camera prompts me to be awake to the unfolding. The photograph, but preceding that, the very act of photographing, points to the thing itself. Drawing from the Buddhist notion of *tathata*, thusness and thatness, Roland Barthes alludes to the nonverbal quality of the photograph. Everything is as it is in the void of the place, in the photograph. "Here it is," a photograph of the landscape, an artifact with its own reality resulting from an experience that has its own immediacy. Travel the same road, and you will also experience the mysteries.

"Lookin' for love in all the wrong places." Turning off County Line Road, I stop and rest in a country cemetery. The names of Irish families are carved on the headstones. In this quiet place, I lie peacefully in the grass. I would be willing to give up much in this life. The farmland stretches out on all sides.

Photographing along these country roads is beginning to have a deeply existential quality. I realize that I am also detached from the landscape. Driving down the roads in my car, I look for something to photograph, and I try to find the hidden meanings as the sun plays its tricks, as my mood changes, as the afternoon passes. More and more frequently, I find myself photographing from the car window, rarely stopping now to compose a shot that takes me far from the car. I am relating to the landscape at the same time that I am separating myself from it. As photographer, I am both participant and observer. In the car with my second eye, I am alienated from that which I desire to be a part of. My project is becoming a metaphor for the existential human condition. As humans, we have separated ourselves from the source of our being. In order to become this special-

ized human species, we have alienated ourselves from the land. My travel on country roads has become an exploration into the human condition—of my being in the world but not of it. This is both a curse and a salvation. In the Eastern sense, this is the challenge. I am the warrior with a camera traveling a road that stretches into the universe. The stars soon will shine as night falls over the prairie.

Photographing from the window of the car, I have entered another reality. My existence is both secular and sacred, as Mircea Eliade notes, two modes of being in the world—in it and beyond it. Photographing in the country has become a religious endeavor, a spiritual experience. Intellectually, I am doing theology in the course of traveling over the land. In bringing the secular and sacred realms together into a single reality, I am engaged in a phenomenology of contemporary existence—experienced and known in the course of a journey. Traveling in this world along the roads of the Midwest is the entering of a sacred space. The landscape that I see is filled with transcendent meaning.

Driving east of town, I turn off Highway 38 and onto Pritchard Road and travel south. Merle Haggard sings on: "I think I'll stay around until I'm sick of home-sweet-home." The driveways of farms lead back into an ordered world of a house, a barn, some sheds, a granary and corncrib, and a silo. The way is lined by trees planted years ago. I stop the car and photograph the farmyard.

The house, with its surrounding yard and farm buildings, is an intimate and sacred world. This inhabited space is in essence a home. A family lives in the world as it dwells in the house and its immediate surroundings. It has taken years to create a place for the soul to dwell. Each farmyard is a unique landscape made first in the selection of the site and then in the building and the planting over the years; it is a habitat for human life. For all those born on the home-stead, this will be the most significant home of their lives. Where we are born is a reference for all that follows, the place that we will continue to call home. Where we might expect to die is the next most significant landmark. In between, we wander from one place to another.

My photographing of the landscape, my search for a vision, has turned out to be a symbol of the existential conflict between stability of place and movement through space. In both our social existence and our cosmic condition, we are pulled between staying and leaving, living and dying, hanging on and giving in. To move on, to become, is to leave something behind. We die to leave and leave to die, and in our leaving and dying we wish to be born again. I travel to find a home.

The American landscape, especially that of the Midwest, symbolizes and exemplifies the contrast between place and space. The phe-nomenologist of the landscape, Yi-Fu Tuan, characterizes the Midwest as a mythical land located at the center of the country but which inspires us to move to another land. Growing up in the Midwest, we are torn between staying at home and moving away in order to become something else. A son or daughter of the middle border carries a lifelong guilt no matter which course is chosen.

Could we be less torn by the conflict be-tween space and place? Must the journey always be away from home? Could not travel be a grow-ing awareness, not of places away from home, but of the newness of home as a place? Is there a way to resolve the conflict between staying and leaving, between place and space? Could there be a road that would take me toward home?

As I travel one of the roads in the northwest corner of the county, Willie Nelson sings "Pre-tend I Never Happened": "I'll be leavin' in the mornin' for a place I hope to find; all the places

must be better than the ones I leave behind." I stop and take from my wallet a worn, folded piece of paper. From the paper, I read a few lines that I have copied from a T. S. Eliot poem: "We shall not cease from exploration / And the end of all our exploring / Will be to arrive where we started / And know the place for the first time." How can I come to know the place?

According to Keiji Nishitani, of the Kyoto School of Japanese Zen philosophy, in his essays on religion and nothingness, we wipe away the boundlessness of space when we allow our-selves to live daily, taking things as they come. By a "dropping off of body and mind," we re-turn to a home where all things are dharma-like, as they really are. Such a mode of being is to arrive at the "home-ground," where all things are completely in harmony with what they actu-ally are and ought to be. It is a "coming home with empty hands," and each being has found its place among all other things. In Zen terms, there is world unity in emptiness, in the full-ness of the homebound existence. The home-ground is an existence free of care and open to the reality of the world. Travel to this place—the home-ground of all things—requires a journey to awareness rather than travel of any geographi-cal distance. Still, it is a journey to a far place.

Willie Nelson sings: "Sometimes it's heaven, and sometimes it's hell, and sometimes I don't even know." I pass another grain elevator, one of the old ones on the line of the Chicago & North Western Railroad. Willie Nelson's song still appeals to me: "Sometimes I take it as far as I can; sometimes I don't even go." The sen-sibility of the song differs from the idea of the sun's rising every morning and the moon's rising every night. The song is immersed in Western fatalism and resignation. Zen finds salvation in emptiness. Yet, the country song touches the modern malaise.

We of the West live in an age of lost meaning. The ethos of the Enlightenment has come to an end. We can no longer believe fully in scientific rationalism as the source of all knowledge and human progress. The Enlightenment liberated us from the tradition of one era only to be captured by the materialistic ethic of another. My travel is a journey through the modern era, an attempt to go beyond it and to travel toward a reconstruction. Below the ruins of modernism, I seek an underground tradition that allows the esoteric realm to enter our daily lives. Although I continue to have my moments of nostalgia for lost meaning, my purpose is to find a new meaning in our postmodern time.

Beyond the existential nihilism that has resulted from the collapse of scientific rationalism and its materialistic culture is the esoteric tradition that is found especially in Eastern philosophy and religion, but which is also found hidden in the Judeo-Christian tradition of the West. My journey is a romantic one in that I live between two eras and wish to find meaning in what I am now experiencing. I wish to rise above the conflict and disorder of the modern condition. I wish to be whole again.

The high-voltage power lines cut through the rich fields, carrying nuclear-generated electricity to Chicago, as I listen to "Friend Don't Take Her She's All I Got." Farmhouses and buildings stand abandoned in the middle of fields that are now cash-cropped by corporate landowners. Rows of corn and soybeans run to the edges of old foundations. Large dairy barns are shedding their sidings, and the post-and-beam structures are exposed like the bony skeletons of giant mastodons. Low and sleek metal sheds replace the wooden farm buildings. The sun is low in the sky; and it is getting too late to take any more photographs. And I am hungry again.

The old landscape, the part of the natural environment that has been shaped by the human presence, is disappearing, and a new one is emerging. The new landscape involves new human relationships and values and an altered relationship to the land. I prefer the landscapes that I have known, but this nostalgia must not obscure what is actually happening around me. We must not, as J. B. Jackson cautions, dwell on the disappearance of the old to the neglect of present-day realities. This is a transitional landscape that I am photographing, but it is also a landscape with its own unique character.

The country roads that I now travel continually cross under or over the state thruway. The land is framed as much by the highways as the homesteads. The roads and highways that run in all directions increasingly determine the look and spirit of the place. As reflected in this Midwest landscape, we are in a time of change and contradiction. All around there is the juxtaposition of the old and the new. Within this landscape is the emergence of a new order. Although the power company and the agribusiness operations are evident in the transformation, a new aesthetic is developing that will affect us in ways yet to be determined.

Among the changes we are experiencing is a recognition of the impermanence of all things, including our own lives. Other ages aimed at permanence and immortality. Our time is increasingly one of transience and mortality. Although we may nostalgically prefer to live in stone houses with Victorian details, it is the cheaply constructed ranch house with the attached garage that serves our needs. The house that we inhabit may not outlast us, but we will likely move to several other houses before we no longer have the need to be sheltered in this world. Devotion to a past with a seemingly permanent order is not only inappropriate for contemporary existence but it is an obstacle to realizing the actuality of our human lives. All is impermanent in this life and in the universe. A Zen poem ends with the line: "Change rules the world forever." My search for a home must be with an awareness of the cosmic fact of impermanence.

North of DeKalb and east of Sycamore I turn onto Old State Road. Parked with its rear end to the road next to an old milkhouse is a public school bus that has been converted into a church-school bus. Printed in large letters on the back of the bus is LUKE 14:23. As soon as I get home, I look up the passage in the Bible. It is Jesus' parable of the great banquet: "Then the master told his servant, 'Go out to the roads and country lanes and make them come in, so that my house may be full.' " There are many, including this traveler, who are on a religious mission.

The seventeenth-century poet Bashō set out near the end of his life on a two-and-a-half-year journey that would take him to the unexplored territory of north of Edo. In *Narrow Road to the Deep North*, Bashō describes the journey that involved the casting away of his possessions and attachments, including the casting away of his own self. As Bashō traveled, he became part of the larger world. A hundred and fifty years later, in Denmark, Søren Kierkegaard also wrote an account of a condition of the self, of the typically Western self that refuses to become part of that which is beyond itself. A "sickness unto death," as Kierkegaard called the condition, is the despair we humans experience when we fail to become part of the otherness of the world. In addition to the increasing awareness of the impermanence of the world, we who travel on this journey come to recognize that this Western, ego-centered self is not only inappropriate and unhealthy but that it denies the nature of the ultimate reality. We travel in eternity, in all the mystery of the universe, and we travel to lose ourselves to the world.

This thing we call the self, the thing to which we are so attached, can come home only when it gives itself up to the world. As Nishitani notes: "This must be a standpoint where one sees one's own self in all things, in living things, in hills and rivers, towns and hamlets, tiles and stones, and loves all these things 'as oneself.' " We, then, are of the landscape, lost (and found) in the absolute emptiness of space. We have arrived at the home place.

In this immediate moment is an eternity. Time and place have been transcended. Time has no beginning and no end. There is an endless compassion in this place beyond all places. We have traveled far through the landscape. Confusion, conflict, and fear will inevitably return as we enter the old landscape of ceaseless thought and judgment, of striving and of the overwhelming sense of the self. Krishnamurti says that time and thought produce the fear we have of this worldly life. Thought creates fear, and thought is the response to a memory of the past. The objective is not to control thought and time but to allow the self to be still, to allow it to be lost beyond time and place. It is only with a compassionate mind, one that is free of fear and free of the preconceptions of the past and the expectations of the future, that we can face reality. It is the only state of being that is in fact reality. Travel on country roads leads to such awareness, to an enlightenment and to ultimate reality. With a quiet mind, I will travel a few more miles before the sun sets.

Willie Nelson sings, "I may be makin' a mistake again, but if I lose or win, how will I know?" I turn off the radio. The land spreads around me in all directions. A red-tailed hawk watches from high on a telephone pole. The beauty just is, and there is no need in the moment to know anything else.

So it is, then, that after years of traveling on other roads and highways, I have returned to the country roads of the Midwest. In looking for something to photograph in the landscape,

I have discovered the importance of watching all things as they rise and pass away, of seeing things in their actuality as they really are. Experiencing the landscape in silence, in bare attention beyond thought, I have become aware of the absolute nothingness of the world and of the reality beyond words, of all that is immeasurable and mysterious. There is great beauty in the harmony perceived in stillness. Life itself, as part of all that is, is an aesthetic dwelling in the world.

The road is a home place in which we may live in eternity. The journey is inward to an unknown place. Home is where I have never been before. Here, now, in this place as I travel, I am at home.

The transcendent quality of the Midwest,
one that survives all human constructions, has to do with the line of the
horizon, the way the sky meets the land, the drift of clouds over the
fields, the way the sun reflects against the weathered barn. This is the
landscape that has brought me back to the Midwest after years of
travel in another place.

DeKalb County, June 1984 (this page and following five pages)

· *A Winter's Tale* ·

SNOW HAS FALLEN AGAIN during the night. The
faint light of the morning sun appears in the gray
sky and climbs up the far edge of the Golden
Years Plaza. In the back yard, black starlings
gather on the power lines near the transformer.
A red squirrel jumps from the oak tree and
moves along the top of the ruined lattice fence
built long ago by a former tenant. As a reminder,
perhaps, of the reality of my existence, I have
kept the old fence behind the house I now call
home. The wind swirls the snow into drifts,
blocking the driveway, and the temperature will
not rise above zero today.

Sometime in the days ahead, the sun will
be brighter, the snow will begin to melt, and a
gentle breeze will warm the land. But now we
are in a special season, the season of the long
winter. It is a time that always seems devoid
of life and renewal. The realization that spring
emerges from the quietness of winter does not
come easily to us. Until the discovery is made
each year, we are in a state of a wintering of the
spirit.

Venturing out to face the bitter wind and to
struggle for a footing in the unshoveled snow
will be difficult this morning. But I need the
walk after days of confinement at home. I also
need a change from this continual reading, a

reading that has taken its own course this winter.
I have stored up quotations, much as the squirrel in the tree has stored up walnuts to provide
sustenance for the season. I have saved quotations such as the one from French philosopher
Jacques Monod: "The ancient alliance has been
destroyed; man knows at last that he is alone in
the universe's indifferent immensity out of which
he emerged only by chance." All my reading
about quantum physics suggests that each discovery serves only to question further the human
ability ever to know the world. Whether in the
universe or in the realm of daily existence, our
primary relation to the world may well be one
of not knowing it. A line from the poet Charles
Wright strikes me: "There is so little to say, and
so much time to say it in."

The deep tracks of schoolchildren guide me
as I make my way through the unplowed street
toward town. Crows fly among the branches of
the tall silver maples in the watertower park.
Already I seem to be entering another realm.
I am becoming aware in a way that I was not
when I first stepped out of the house. I think of
Thoreau, the wanderer, who let life flow as he
attended to his immediate surroundings. I will
let this day be a journey of sorts, a wandering
journey.

Remembering the walking meditation exercise of the Zen master Thich Nhat Hanh, I concentrate for the moment on my breath as I inhale and exhale into the cold morning air. As he instructs, I practice lengthening the breath for several minutes, and for several steps I focus entirely on the words "My heart is now at peace." Eventually the mind wanders, and I begin to observe this wandering mind as another event in the morning landscape.

Cars and trucks move slowly along Lincoln Highway, DeKalb's main street. Two blind men, their white aluminum canes darting out in front of them, move along the edge of the highway and find the entrance to Andy's Bar. The front window at Dot's Place is steamed over from the breakfasts that have been fried for truckers since 3:00 A.M. A patrolman, having taken a coffee break, returns to his car. Deciding not to stop in at Dot's, I make my way to the university to pick up the accumulated mail. As the limestone gothic tower of Altgeld Hall rises from behind the willows surrounding the lagoon, I delight in the moment.

"We must begin not from metaphysics," the Indian philosopher Ravi Ravindra observes, "but from experience, recognizing ourselves as we are: disintegrated, confused and without will, like chaff driven by the wind." And he instructs that as we begin to wake up, to become mindful, we are no longer at peace, for peace is for those who are either sound asleep or fully awake. "In between is the struggle: a step forward, a relapse, a fall, another moment of seeing—the unknown playing hide-and-seek with the known." In the experience of the present, rather than in explanation, I am seeking a spiritual path that begins where I am at this moment, in this place, at this time, as I wander the streets of this midwestern town.

I stop this morning at Rog's Tap, by reputation the roughest bar in town. Several men sit at the bar, hovering over their drinks in the darkness of a room warmed by colored lights advertising Budweiser, Schlitz, and Old Style. Sitting at the window, I watch aging passengers as they carry their white-bagged lunches from McDonald's to the Continental Golden Charter bus. The western-bound Chicago & North Western freight train speeds past the old station. On the jukebox, John Conlee sings his song "Nothing Behind You (and Nothing in Sight)":

Ain't that a hell of a way
to live out your life
knowing all your tomorrows
will be just alike.
When the worries have stolen
the dreams from your nights,
and there's nothing behind you
and nothing in sight.

The lyrics remind me that there is something I need to look for at the DeKalb Public Library.

•

The gray morning clouds have passed, and now the sun shines brightly against the soft, brown stone of the town's library. During the holidays, my visiting daughter has suggested that sometime I read William Wordsworth's narrative poem "The Ruined Cottage." We had been talking about our common condition of being observers of the world as we move from one place to another. The poem, I soon find, is about the wandering poet who meets an aging peddler, a fellow traveler on the road. Upon meeting, the old man says to the poet:

I see around me here
Things which you cannot see. We die, my Friend
Nor we alone, but that which each man loved
And prized in his peculiar nook of earth
dies with him, or is changed, and very soon
Even of the good is no memorial left.

The peddler then tells "a tale of silent suffering," a story about the woman Margaret who once lived in the cottage and longed for the return of her husband. The peddler describes how Margaret's hope for her husband's return slowly bends and breaks her spirit and finally destroys her life.

What are we to make of life's suffering, the poet wonders, in which such things happen. It is the contemplative mind, the peddler notes, that creates sympathies that "grow with thought." Gone is the husband Robert, who once "dwelt in the poor cottage" and stood "and whistled many a snatch of merry tunes / That had no mirth in them." And gone is Margaret: "She is dead, / And nettles rot and adders sun themselves / Where we have sat together while she nursed / Her infant at her breast." The peddler had observed all this: "A wanderer among the cottages, / I with my pack of winter raiment saw / The hardships of that season." All human artifacts are quietly absorbed into the natural world—while we the wandering observers "thus disturb / The calm of Nature with our restless thoughts." One who wanders from place to place, confronting the mysteries of nature, finds little consolation in creeds or in the thoughts of the inquiring mind.

I wander out of the library, Wordsworth's "dreamer among men, indeed / An idle dreamer," who in the thought endures the things that are beheld at home. Yet it is with this thoughtful mind, rather than with the desire for worldly achievement, that the wanderer travels an inner way toward union with the transcendent. The meaning of my worldly existence lies in the experiencing of the holy other in everyday life. The Way, as the Eastern-trained psychotherapist Karlfreid Dürckheim observes, "is the never-ending practice which leads us from the reality that was shaped by our world-ego to the reality that is beyond time and space, and thence towards transparence and new becoming." I wander to end this separation from the wholeness of essential being. I practice ceaselessly to be on the path that leads to wholeness. The wanderer never arrives but is always on the way.

Directly across from the library is the low brick building that is the Ronan-Moore Mortuary. I pass the building quickly. It is getting late, and I have not had lunch, and what is a day without at least one stop at Sullivan's? A bumper sticker on a rusted Cutlass Supreme parked at the curb near the library proclaims One Nuclear Bomb Can Ruin Your Day. Farther down the street, another sticker on a GMC pickup truck reads Support Hog Prices—Run Over a Chicken. "Life," Ralph Waldo Emerson writes, "is our dictionary," and books "are for the scholar's idle times." When we "can read God directly," Emerson says," the hour is too precious to be wasted in other men's transcripts of their readings." Emerson adds: "The office of the scholar is to cheer, to raise, and to guide men by showing them facts amidst appearance. He plies the slow, unhonored, and unpaid task of observation." No hour is lost that is spent on the street—or at Sullivan's Tavern.

At the tavern, Shorty, of Hiatt Plumbing and Heating, is already making his afternoon stop at the bar. The four Sullivan brothers are briskly serving the afternoon crowd. A bowl of homemade chili would be just right, with some packaged crackers on the side. Having seen me enter, Albert brings me an Augsburger. I hear a man tell his friend that his spirits would rise ten degrees if it would only warm up a bit.

The old man next to me is drinking his whiskey and beer. He says to me, "I get up late in the morning and walk uptown to get a newspaper. Sometimes I walk over to the lagoon and watch the ducks." He then adds, "We have to have some beauty in life." Finishing his beer and shot of whiskey, he prepares to return to his room to take a nap before watching television until bedtime.

The peddler in Wordsworth's poem says of Margaret:

She loved this wretched spot, nor would for worlds
Have parted hence; and still the length of road,

And this rude bench, one torturing hope endeared,
Fast rooted at her heart. And here, my friend,
In sickness she remained; and here she died,
Last human tenant of these ruined walls.

Before leaving, the old man asks, "But what am I to do? And I can't see so good anymore." Knowing that I am moved by his question, he puts on his cap and coat and leaves the bar before I can respond.

The world, certainly my world, remains an unknowable mystery. I do not have a Newtonian model of a world governed by a universal plan that is reducible to scientific laws. If absolute truth exists, it is inaccessible to the human mind. "Whatever we call reality," the Nobel scientist Ilya Prigogine observes, "is revealed to us only through the active construction in which we participate." I am firmly placed inside the truth, and I am its participant. The world is thus open to an understanding from within. A philosopher of science, Herman Weyl, points to the location of our interpretation: "This inner awareness of myself is the basis for the understanding of my fellowmen whom I meet and acknowledge as beings of my own kind, with whom I communicate sometimes so intimately as to share joy and sorrow with them." And this inner awareness is part of everything that is, and everything that is transcendent in the world. From where do we come, then, into this nothingness, this everything? Loren Eiseley proposes an answer: "Out of a dark hat in a closet called Night."

•

Darkness comes early these winter days. I walk home through the narrow alleys that run north and south behind the numbered streets. Barns and garages and work sheds left from another age line the alleys. Off First Street, I wander into the back door of Barb City Manor. Elderly women and a few elderly men are coming out of their rooms into the long hallway. Tables in the cafeteria are being set up for the evening meal. I wonder what wintering is at this time of life.

Wandering this day, as in an entire life, has been a search for home, for a return to wholeness in the world. In the solitude of this day of wandering, I have gone into the world in order to leave it, and in leaving it, I have found others on the way. "To leave the 'world,'" Thomas Merton writes, "is to leave oneself first of all and to begin to live for others." The solitary wanderer, instead of being isolated, loses the self to a larger self of others. The wanderer becomes a part of the universe, even (and especially) in this little town of DeKalb. And in the wandering I enter another place, a transcendent place, as I return to the house I sometimes in the night call home. I know that my true home is not a place bound by walls. It is an inner place beyond this world of self and all its seeking. We come home to nothingness, to all that is. I know that I will never in the world be at home in the world.

It is nighttime, and gusts of snow-filled wind blow against the windows of the old house. I have earned my living this day wandering through the town and visiting its haunts. What is left is the accounting. Thoreau went to his cabin at Walden Pond to write a sacred text about the experiment of living. And the writing of the text, as Stanley Cavell notes in his treatise of *Walden*, was an act of awakening, and thus an act that was also a losing of the self. A writer deliberately lives a way that can be expressed in the writing. But in the faithful reporting, in writing the news of the world we have made and prophetically of the one that might be, the writer lives to be lost in the moment of the expression. I write in solitude into the wintering night.

Entering a secret place, I find a silence and intimacy in a meditation on the original experience of the day. This is an entering into "death's space," as the French literary critic Maurice Blanchot calls it. "The writer, then, is one who writes in order to be able to die, and he is one whose power to write comes from an anticipated relation with death." When one writes, one dies in the moment of expression. All is lost when it is given up to the expressed word. We write to be able to die; and we die to be able to write.

Writing is an emptying of the mind. It is a creating of a silent space that is devoid of facts and fears and confusion. Writing is a release to the silence that is truly the sacred. "When there is silence," Krishnamurti observes, "there is immense, timeless space; then and only then is there a possibility of coming upon that which is the eternal, sacred." Finally, as one dies in the last words, "the mind is absolutely free and silent and one discovers that which is beyond all words, which is timeless." The observer has become the observed, the self is lost, and there is no division between this world and any other. "That," Krishnamurti says, "is what death means—ending, complete ending; and when there is complete ending, something new is born."

Ultimately we are opened to a space that transcends all thoughts and words. The truth is beyond any human expression. We have moved beyond time, as Martin Heidegger suggests we might, in a releasement of ourselves from the material world. The eternal is in the present, without beginning or end in time. Thus Ludwig Wittgenstein observes: "If we take eternity to mean not infinite temporal duration but timelessness, then eternal life belongs to those who live in the present." As I look up from my night of writing, the clock tells me that three hours have passed, and my experiencing of this time has seemed only a moment. In my writing, in my dying, time has stood still. I have been only in the present moment; I have experienced eternity.

"And, ere the stars were visible," Wordsworth writes, ending his tale. The wandering poet and the peddler then "attained / A rustic inn, our evening resting place." Now I lay me down to sleep, a wintering soul tonight to keep. Another day I have lived and died. In the morning I will awake, born again to winter's new day.

*S*ometime in the days ahead,
the sun will be brighter, the snow will begin to melt, and a
gentle breeze will warm the land. But now we are in a special
season, the season of the long winter. It is a time that always seems
devoid of life and renewal. The realization that spring emerges
from the quietness of winter does not come easily to us. Until the
discovery is made each year, we are in a state of a
wintering of the spirit.

DeKalb, December 1985 (this page and following three pages)

· *The Journey East* ·

I WILL TELL the story the way it happened. But even then, what I tell is still happening, and the events are being re-created as I write. A recent letter from a fellow traveler answered a question I had asked near the end of the journey. I had asked her, as in a Zen koan, whether it was necessary to travel. I had quoted from the *Tao Te Ching*:

> Without going out of my door
> I know all things on earth.
> Without looking out of my window
> I can know the ways of heaven.
>
> For the further one travels
> The less one knows.
>
> The sage therefore
> Arrives without traveling,
> Sees all without looking,
> Does all without doing.

She answered: "It seems we are always traveling as a part of living, although we become most conscious of this only when we arrive or depart, when we are attuned to or watchful of things newly seen." She added, "I will miss you as a traveling companion."

•

Preparations for the trip to China were simple and few. I read the briefing materials supplied to the twenty-five delegates who would investigate law and justice in several cities and provinces of China. In Providence for the month of June, I walked the evenings with friends and family on the shores of Goosewing Beach. I learned to play a piano rendition of Frank Loesser's "On a Slow Boat to China" and watched Willie Nelson's videotape about the songwriter: "Write it down—what you found—songwriter. Don't let it all slip away. . . . Someone is listening today." I read a book of love poems by Chinese women of the early dynasties. I sat with Cambodian monks at the Khmer Buddhist Temple and listened to the Dharma talks of Maha Ghosananda.

My objective in making the trip to China was not altogether clear. After all, as Chuang Tzu had written over two thousand years ago, "The good traveler doesn't know where he's going. / The great traveler doesn't know where he's been." When asked, I replied simply that I was going to China to see what it is like to go to China. To observe the elusive legal system in three weeks' time would be like, according to the Chinese aphorism, "looking at flowers from a galloping horse." The trip would be a continuation of my own attempt to bring Eastern ideas and practices into everyday life.

"All that we are is a result of what we have thought," *The Dhammapada* begins. I was taking care of what I was thinking. I also was practicing awareness of the changing nature of all things and realizing the sorrow that comes from an attachment to all that is impermanent. I would travel with patience, watching the flow of all things of which I am a part. Before leaving, I happened to read a Taoist poem:

> Picking chrysanthemums by the east hedge
> I can see the hills to the south a long way away:
> It is sunset and the air over the mountains is
>   beautiful:
> Birds are flying in flocks back to their nests.
> This tastes real.
> I would like to talk about it, but there are
>   no words.

I have, fortunately, gazed my life away, and the telling is only a faint portrait of what I have seen.

•

High over the Midwest, jet engines roaring through the clouds, the airplane takes me on the first of the many flights on this trip. "In the place where we are now," Alan Watts once said, "we have already arrived." What we are seeking is already here, and I am on the move again. Everyday life is a great mystery, and only now am I beginning to live fully with this realization. There is a dull stillness within the drone of the engines. Quoting the Third Chinese Patriarch of Zen, "The Great Way is not difficult for those who have no preferences," I write a postcard to a friend as we fly over Illinois. There is peace in emptiness in the realm of the sacred. The airplane descends through the clouds and rolls smoothly down the runway to the San Francisco terminal.

Maha Ghosananda had once asked, "What is the giant to be killed?" and I answered, "Time." On this flight, as well as on the others, there is a sense of timelessness. Where, after all, could one be going when there is no place to go? *The Diamond Sutra* had prepared me for this journey to the East: "Dwell nowhere, and bring forth that mind."

We spend the night in the San Francisco Hilton located in Chinatown. Our delegation meets for the first time in the late afternoon. We introduce ourselves, and our leaders tell us about the experiences of past delegations. Already it appears that we are disparate characters coming together in a common venture that will join us in unexpected ways. No better moment than now to practice mindfulness, to be patient and observant, and to help others on the way to realization as the trip to China unfolds. My travel roommate and I have dinner at a Chinese restaurant, practicing the chopsticks that will be used throughout our travel.

Back in my hotel room, I find in the drawer of my bedside table a copy of *The Teaching of Buddha*, placed next to the Gideon Bible. I ring Housekeeping and am told that I may take the copy with me to China. Early in the morning, elderly Chinese women gracefully practice Tai Chi on the second-floor walkway outside the hotel. The two reality principles—the dark and the light, the *yin* and the *yang*—are being balanced as morning comes. That the harmony of the universe might be found in oneself, as one becomes part of the nameless and the unknowable, part of all that is: "I do not know its name, I call it Tao." We repack our suitcases, meet the bus at the lobby door, and return to the airport where we board the large 747 that will take us to Tokyo, and then, after a brief stop, on to Beijing.

•

Trees line the narrow road from the Beijing airport into the city. In the middle of the night, we pass slow-moving bicycles in the yellow misty light of street lamps as the bus makes its way to the guest hotel. Horse-drawn wagons for the collection of night soil are making their rounds. In an essay on Buddhist ethics, it has been written, "We are all of us interrelated—not just people, but animals too, and stones, clouds, trees." In the silence of the night, a secret word is spoken. The way is open to all beings, all things.

In the morning, we make our visit to the United States Embassy. Among the balsam poplars of Ritan Park, where cicadas sing into the moist air, we walk to the compound, cameras ready to record our first steps into China. Seated in the large room, fans churning overhead, our delegation is immediately eager to ask questions. Embassy officials have their own concerns: apprehension about economic reforms, anxiety regarding relations between China and Russia, and fear of another cultural revolution. And here in the Middle Kingdom, we also are being watched by a conscience much older than that of the West. While we seek facts and information, there is a search beyond all of this: "Within Siddhartha there slowly grew and ripened the knowledge of what wisdom really was and the goal of his long seeking. It was nothing but a preparation of the soul, a capacity, a secret art of thinking, feeling, and breathing thoughts of unity at every moment of life." At this first session in China, I think of no question that can be asked.

In the afternoon, we begin our meetings with Ministry of Justice officials; the meetings will be repeated in similar settings and fashion throughout our visit. Some of us are seated around the large table, and others sit in the stuffed chairs at the edges of the room. The covered teacups have already been set at our places. Soon young women come carrying enormous thermos bottles and pour hot water into the cups. The leading official begins his prepared statement.

Our translator relays something of the message as it is presented. Very shortly, our delegation is ready to break in with questions that will make sense from the Western experience: "How much crime is there in China?" "What are the causes of your crime?" "Are there guarantees of due process in Chinese law?" "What about alcoholism and drug addiction?" There seems to be little correspondence between the questions and the answers. They are being misunderstood and mistranslated—English to Chinese and back again to English—and there is a wide gap between the assumptions of our questions and the reality of Eastern social existence. My listening turns to the sounds of the language and the songs of the cicadas that now fill the room. The truth is somewhere beyond this ceaseless search for knowledge. Later in the evening, a few of us walk through Tiananmen Square and watch the children and families in quiet play. Night hawks fall from the dark sky. I walk home to nowhere.

It is early morning. Slow-moving bicycles fill the streets of Beijing. I reach for *The Teaching of Buddha* and turn to the section titled "Human Defilements." The passage reads: "There are two kinds of worldly passion that defile and cover the purity of Buddha-nature. The first is the passion for analysis and discussion by which people become confused in judgment. The second is the passion for emotional experience by which people's values become confused."

In a few minutes, we will be ready to get into the bus and head for another formal meeting, this time investigating the Chinese legal system. On the way to the meeting place, we park at the Memorial Hall and file past the body of Chairman Mao. Outside, straw-hatted workers dig in piles of sand; cranes rise high above scaffolded cement office towers. We move on, desiring answers and more experience.

The sounds of the cicada float out of the willows as we walk through Beihai Park to lunch in the ancient pavilion. Lotus plants fill the lagoon and rowboats drift across the lake. Lunch will be an elegant serving of many exotic dishes. We gather at the round table and share from the center. Beer and orange soda are continually poured into our glasses. "*Xie, Xie,*" we offer our thanks and depart through the latticed gates of red, green, and gold. The white-marbled Dagoba Temple rises above the park.

Throughout our days of meetings, dining, and touring, I continue to be aware that reality is beyond the knowing mind. Especially in the objective thinking of the inquisitive mind, we are set apart from what we are observing, therefore missing the essence of reality. To be in contact with our Buddha-nature is to be a part of what we experience. We are in the process of awakening, of becoming enlightened beings, when we realize our attachment to the knowing mind. The awakened mind is free and craves nothing; it is watchful of all that is here and now.

I hand *The Dhammapada* to a friend as we approach the Temple of Heaven, and we read: "Find joy in watchfulness; guard well your mind. Uplift yourself from the lower self, even as an elephant draws himself out of a muddy swamp." Meditatively, without choice, with what Buddhists call "choiceless awareness," we quietly enter the circular Hall of Prayer for Good Harvests. In watchfulness we behold the greatest treasure, the mystery of complete awareness.

At the Beijing airport, on our way to Inner Mongolia, a young schoolgirl approaches as we sit waiting for our flight to be called. She asks me, "From where do you come?" I answer, and then she tells us that she is in the lobby to practice her English with foreign visitors. We learn that someday she will be a translator for an agency of the Chinese government. After a delay caused by the hot night air, we board the propeller airplane to Hohhot. Each of us is handed a paper fan for the takeoff. As we rise into the sky, condensation from the air system appears like smoke above us. We fan rapidly into the night sky as the plane flies north over the Great Wall.

•

Carved around the base of the Five-Pagoda Temple in Hohhot is *The Diamond Sutra* in three languages: Mongolian, Tibetan, and Sanskrit. We climb to the top of the temple and view the old town. Many of the Buddha carvings on the temple have been damaged during the Cultural Revolution. But now the government, with the guidance of the Chinese Buddhist Association, is restoring the temples throughout China. In the afternoon, we visit a neighborhood police station and ask more questions about crime in China. Unlike police in Western societies, neighborhood police in China make few arrests; their daily activities are devoted to crime prevention and to education.

In a nearby village, a few miles to the north, we have a formal meeting with a mediation committee. Walking out onto the dirt road in front of the low, gray, brick building with a tiled roof, I watch the villagers who have gathered at the corner to watch our deliberations. An old man with a thin, white beard and a blue Mao cap on his head cautiously approaches me and puts the lens of the camera to his eye and looks deeply into it. Then he looks up at me and smiles.

In the morning, we are in the bus and on an excursion north over the Daqing Mountains to the grasslands of Inner Mongolia. Our tourist guide, a Mongolian herdsman, comes galloping over the horizon of China's frontier. He sings a native song as he dismounts and enters the bus. We are shown a ritual site on the top of a low hill; the plains spread out in all directions and are dotted by a few adobe farmsteads. Back in the village, we walk into the courtyard of the beautiful, brightly colored lama summer temple of the Living Buddha. Inside, an aging lama appears out of a dark corner and at the altar chants an ancient scripture. We place coins at the foot of the altar. As the others depart in search of a yurt for the night, I remain for a while sitting half-lotus in the meditation hall of the temple. Later in the evening, we dine on mutton cooked in hot pots, and we are toasted lavishly by our hosts from the Inner Mongolian Autonomous Region.

•

On the two-thousand-mile flight to the far western province of Xinjiang, my seatmate and I read parts of *The Dhammapada*. We all have made the overnight trip from Hohhot to Beijing on a train pulled by a steam locomotive that could be seen from our car as it rounded bends of the river along the mountain-ridged valley. On a trip such as this, a trip taken by scholars in search of knowledge, there is much talk and there is, likewise, the opportunity to be very careful with words and with the actions that go with the words. *The Dhammapada* counsels that "better than a thousand useless words is one single word that gives peace." And then: "The holy spend not idle words on things of desire. When pleasure or pain comes to them, the wise feel above pleasure and pain." When we arrive in Urumqi, there will be luggage to sort, seats on the bus to be chosen, and rooms for the night to be selected. Can we human beings live at peace in the confusion and conflict of our daily lives? A. J. Muste has said, "There is no way to peace; peace is the way." The way is to be practiced on a journey to the far corners of China.

The next day we go high into the Tianshan Mountains to the Heavenly Lake. Late in the afternoon, we wearily return from a hot and dusty ride across the desert. Near the edge of the city, we stop at a farming village to investigate the process of mediation. The people of Badon village carefully watch us as we climb out of the bus and gather around tables placed beside the long, white-sided house. Overhead, ripening grapes hang from an arbor that extends the length of the house. Tea is poured and watermelon slices are served. Zinnias are in full

bloom in the nearby garden. Children in bright dress clothes watch our proceedings from a distant doorway. An occasional swallow darts in and out of the house window. Incense burns from under the eaves.

We are welcomed by the township chair. In translation, she acknowledges our tiredness from the long day's journey. The head of the village mediation committee greets us and begins his prepared remarks. The village is composed of a thousand households of different ethnic groups: Han, Hui, Uygur, and Kazakh. After elaborating on the ways of mediation, he concludes by telling us about the increase in agricultural production in the village.

Members of our delegation then begin to quiz our hosts, aggressively asking the questions that have been repeated at similar gatherings throughout the trip. Sitting at the table and listening to the inquiry and attempting to take notes for the delegation, I find my mind wandering back to the passage from *The Teaching of Buddha* on the worldly passion for analysis and discussion and for emotional experience. Sitting under the arbor in the Chinese village and exchanging sounds and glances are experiences beyond concrete understanding. We are left with an impression of what it is like at this point in our human history to spend a late afternoon together in a Chinese village. Our meeting is adjourned, and we are taken on a walk around the village. This is followed by a dinner prepared for us by the villagers. I write a lasting impression in my notebook:

> Evening under the grape arbor,
> Seeking to know the ways
> Of Han, Hui, Uygur, and Kazakh—
> Children watch from a distance.

The mind is always occupied with something. It is like a monkey, always restless and chattering, always moving from one thing to another. Thus the religions of the East employ some form of meditation to quiet the mind, to allow the mind to move beyond conditioned thought. In his *Notebook*, Krishnamurti writes, "To be empty, completely empty, is not a fearsome thing; it is absolutely essential for the mind to be unoccupied, to be empty, unenforced, for then only can it move into unknown depths." Meditation is an examination of reality in a deeper sense while in a quiet state of being, feeling at the same moment one's way into the mystery of existence. It is the entering of a sacred silence, one in which thought and being have become one. Meditation becomes a form of everyday life. In another place, Krishnamurti writes:

> The purpose of life is to *live*—not in the utter chaos and confusion that we call living—but in an entirely different way, to live a life that is full, to live a life that is complete, to live that way today. That is the true meaning of life—to live, not heroically, but to live so complete, inwardly, without fear, without struggle and without all the rest of the misery.

The dry, dusty air of Urumqi produces an allergic reaction that requires me to remain in the hotel for the rest of our stay in Xinjiang province. The guest hotel has the look of a monastery. I welcome the opportunity to be alone in the spacious room while the rest of the delegation goes on a two-day sightseeing trip to Tulufan. I wash clothes and later walk slowly down the wide hallway over the polished yellow and brown floor tiles. Well-worn oriental carpets cover the lobby of the aging hotel. For long periods, I sit at the desk in my room, being nothing and living directly in the moment.

This longing of the heart asks simply for a reconciliation with all that remains mysterious and unknowable. It is not necessary for me to exist only in the realm of the known; I seem to welcome the mystery of the unknown. The

world is essentially unknowable, including this everyday life, and the mystery can be lived in all of its sacred possibilities: in quietness, humility, and solitude. I read in the stillness of my room the words of *The Dhammapada*: "Whereas if a man speaks but a few holy words and yet he lives the life of those words, free from passion and hate and illusion—with right vision and a mind free, craving nothing both now and hereafter—the life of this man is a life of holiness."

•

It rains gently in Shanghai the days we are there. At night the brightly lit boats along the Huangpu River reflect on the water and into the mist as we walk the Bund. Couples openly show their affection for one another. We are told in meetings that the streets of Shanghai are now free of crime and prostitution. The old era of slums, opium dens, and starvation virtually ended with the reforms brought about in 1949 by the People's Republic of China.

In the Shanghai Mental Hospital, we see the suffering that still exists. And for the crime that now exists, an official tells us that "outside influences cause people to make themselves satisfied without regard for others." All over the city, billboards advertise consumer goods: television sets, motorbikes, kitchen appliances, and cameras. "Red-eye disease" afflicts those who desire more than they can afford. Returning in the bus to the Peace Hotel from the banquet of many dishes, we listen while our guide from Shanghai sings for us "We Shall Not Be Moved."

•

As we land on the outskirts of Fuzhou, the coastal capital of Fujian province, water buffaloes pull wooden plows through rice fields. High on Drum Hill, Buddhist pavilions and temples are being repaired and rebuilt. We visit an autoworks factory commune and witness the mediation of a dispute between a mother-in-law and daughter-in-law. The Confucian ethic of respect for parents and elders prevails.

At the evening banquet, we are served elaborate dishes of meat, fowl, fish, and seafood. Vegetables, we are told, are reserved for everyday fare among the townspeople. A government official from the Ministry of Justice is seated at each table. Afterward, I walk to the nearby hotel for overseas Chinese visitors and purchase a volume of the poetry of Wang Wei. In one of his poems, he writes:

> Since I vowed to follow a vegetarian diet,
> I have no more entanglements with worldly
>   affairs.
> I regard the fame and honor of officialdom as
>   superficial,
> I live as I please, unshackled by external fetters.

Even in this far province, I seek a remove from the material objects of this earthly existence.

●

The *yin/yang* principle of balance as a grounding for life increasingly plays on the minds of several of us. Early in the morning, at each of our stops, we have seen Tai Chi exercises being practiced. At this far point in our travel, now in Guangzhou, we feel the predominance of the *yang*—growth and expansion—to the neglect of the *yin* of contraction and rest.

But care must be taken not to become attached to the esoteric ways. *The Teaching of Buddha* cautions us: "Do not become attached to the things you like, do not maintain aversion to the things you dislike. Sorrow and bondage come from one's likes and dislikes." This means that one must take care not to become attached even to Buddhism. There is instead the middle path that leads neither to the desire for things of the earth nor for things of heaven. In Zen Buddhism, there is the expression, "If you meet the Buddha on the road, kill him!" The life of the enlightened being, then, is free of all craving, in-cluding the desire for enlightenment. Only then are we open to the naked mystery of the world. The meditative practice is to keep focused on the present. In *The Teaching of Buddha*, we read the passage, "The secret of health for both mind and body is not to mourn for the past, not to worry about the future, or not to anticipate troubles, but to live wisely and earnestly for the present."

In Guangzhou our delegation is housed in the luxurious White Swan Hotel. We are located across the Pearl River on Shamian Island, once the British enclave made notoriously famous during the Opium Wars. Signs in the compound of large Victorian buildings once warned No Chinese and Dogs Allowed. Our hosts tell us that we are being shown that a developing China can afford an elegant hotel. Traffic moves along the river as we play among the luxuries of the White Swan. During a Sunday morning session with the prosecutor of economic crimes, I write a short poem:

> Bridge over the River Pearl—
> Among the ruins
> The great white bird nests.
> High upon her back
> We watch ancient boats
> Speed toward another shore.

Soon we will take the three-hour train ride to Hong Kong.

●

Over the Pacific, flying backward in time from Hong Kong to San Francisco, we watch as James Stewart pursues the elusive Kim Novak in *Vertigo*. We see the lights of Tokyo from the left windows of the airplane as darkness appears for only a short period of the flight. The man next to me, as we near San Francisco and awaken from sleep, tells me that he is a Chinese Buddhist now studying as an engineer in Philadelphia. In his own life, he is trying to integrate what he calls the "passive" aspects of Buddhism with the active life of the West. But he cautions, "Always be attentive to the suffering that comes with the desires of human existence." That suffering can be stopped by the right practices is the note on which we depart as we walk through Customs.

With some waiting, then a flight to Denver, then on to Chicago, and finally a Greyhound bus ride to DeKalb, I find myself walking down South Third Street toward home. The sun now is shining brightly, and a cool morning breeze stirs a sweet, grassy scent into the air. On the bus, the lines of Chuang Tzu have advised me on how far I might want to go in understanding and in explaining my trip to China:

If you persist in reasoning
About what cannot be understood,
You will be destroyed
By the very thing you seek.

I will continue to live in the mystery that is always present in the unknown. The truth is already here, in this very moment, in this very place. An orange and black monarch butterfly flutters across my path and flies among the lilac bushes. This life, although in many ways simple, is a mystery that I welcome with each day's journey.

*T*o be in contact with our Buddha-nature
is to be a part of what we experience. We are in the process of
awakening, of becoming enlightened beings, when we realize our
attachment to the knowing mind. The awakened mind is free and craves
nothing; it is watchful of all that is
here and now.

Arriving in Fuzhou, China, July 1985

Drum Hill, Fuzhou

Autoworks factory commune

Nursery at autoworks factory commune

Hong Kong

· *A Dark Voyage* ·

DARKNESS HAD COME by late afternoon. Wind was beating against the windows as the weather report on the radio announced, "Gale force winds tonight from Slyne Head to Malin Head." It was my first night in the farmhouse north of Galway. Earlier in the day I had driven from Dublin, and I had spent the afternoon learning how to tend to the house.

I would be here alone for two weeks until Valerie and Anne arrived. Each night the wind would blow across Lake Corrib and over the fields and stone fences to the farmhouse. A calendar on the wall, picturing an ancient monastery, provided an eighth-century verse for January:

> Fierce is the wind tonight
> It ploughs up the white hair of the sea
> I have no fear the Viking hosts
> Will come over the water to me.

I filled the kitchen stove with coal and turf and went upstairs to the cold bed.

·

A year ago, I applied for a Fulbright lectureship to University College Galway. Now as I drive the ten miles in the morning darkness to the univer-sity, I wonder where my journey here will lead. At the university, I am welcomed and asked why I have come. I ask myself, "What is my work here, my mission, perhaps?" Later in the day, after returning to the house, I walk down the road to the ruined monastery of Annaghdown. In the sixth century, Saint Brendan had founded the monastery, and it is told that he is buried there. Walking in the rubble of the monastery, I wonder about Saint Brendan's voyage, a voyage that took him from these shores of Ireland to as far as Greenland and Newfoundland.

In the evening, I read the ninth-century account of Brendan's journey, translated from the Latin as *The Voyage of Saint Brendan*. Before departing, Saint Brendan had declared, "I have resolved in my heart if it is God's will—and only if it is—to go in search of the Promised Land." He set sail in a small boat with several monks and traveled the rough seas. His constant inspiration was Christ's assurance to the disciples as danger threatened their boat on the Sea of Galilee: "Do not be afraid!" Centuries later, I too search for inspiration and a mission, for something beyond this self of mine. Perhaps this is why I am here, in Annaghdown, near Saint Brendan.

I had thought also that a trip to Ireland would

put me close to my Celtic ancestors. My great-grandparents, John Quinney and Bridget O'Keefe, had come from here, emigrating in the 1840s, during the famine. In some ways, I have been a product of their search for a new home in a strange land. My wanderings began long ago in their emigration from Ireland. Some understanding of their life here might help me to be at home in another place. Such an understanding would be part of the quest to end the suffering of the individualized self, to become one with the world. How is the mind, with its heart, to attend to this ultimate quest?

I had brought a few lines with me from *The Dhammapada* and had taped them above the worktable beside the fireplace.

> All things have the nature of mind.
> Mind is the chief and takes the lead.
> If the mind is clear, whatever you do or say
> Will bring happiness that will follow you
> Like your shadow.

As I sit alone in the long evenings, I try to be mindful and let things take their natural course. Such a mind should become still in any place. The Buddhist monk Achaan Chah says, "You will reach a point where the heart tells you what to do."

Yet I find that after a week in the house, it is difficult for me to be comfortably alone in a new, strange place. Away from the familiar surroundings of home and friends, it is hard to be mindful and to watch without judgment all that is now so unfamiliar and uncertain. Each night before bedtime, I listen to one of the meditation tapes and try to practice the acceptance of thoughts as they come and go. I know that suffering comes from attachment to all that is conditioned in my life. And still I experience the suffering as fear and loneliness in this moment. I will continue to practice.

At the university, I am to teach a large lecture course on modern social thought. As I stand at the window of my office, overlooking the river that flows to Galway Bay, gulls fly on the gusts of a rainy wind and glide down to the river's surface. The rising sun momentarily breaks through the dark clouds. Shortly I will tell the class that we are here together to think about modern thought, but also that we are to think about the process of thought itself.

In the class, I ask students to consider their own thoughts as a part of modern thought. I say that thought is not reserved for academicians, as the textbook implies. Eventually, as the weeks pass, we begin to question the modern mode of rational thought. We turn to non-Western thought, to the ideas contained in Hinduism and Buddhism, and we explore the perennial philosophy that is hidden within Western thought. I suggest that Max Weber's struggle with rationalization, his acceptance of it, in spite of his fears about its consequences, combined with his inability to imagine an alternative, led to his mental breakdown. I talk about the modern dualistic mind and suggest a Taoist integration of the polarities into a unified whole. The lessons are brought close to home when we talk about the divided mind in a materialistic society, a mind that necessarily requires a spiritual existence as well. We investigate the high rate of schizophrenia in the west of Ireland. I suggest that the issues raised in the course touch the everyday lives of us all.

Near the end of the course, I write on the blackboard a line from the *Lankavatara Sutra*: "One's teaching is a transgression, for the truth transcends words." This period of my life, now being lived in Ireland, has finally come to this: how to apprehend the truth that is beyond the intellect, beyond words, in the realm of the divine? And how will this affect the nature of my academic and intellectual work? If the truth is beyond the activity of the rational mind, how is this truth to be expressed to the intellectual community? Is it necessary at all to communicate in the traditional form of the reasoned and written word? I will attend to the matter as I journey in the land of my Celtic ancestors.

In his book *The Irish*, Sean O'Faolain says that a sense of the Otherworld has dominated the Celtic imagination through the centuries, with this imagination seeking "a synthesis between dream and reality, aspiration and experience, a shrewd knowledge of the world and a strange reluctance to cope with it, and tending always to find the balance not in an intellectual synthesis but in the rhythm of a perpetual emotional oscillation." The next day in class, I read aloud a passage from W. B. Yeats, from an introduction to the fairy stories he gathered in the west of Ireland: "I have always sought to bring my mind close to the mind of Indian and Japanese poets, old women in Connacht, mediums in Soho, lay brothers whom I imagine dreaming in some medieval monastery the dreams of their village, learned authors who refer all to antiquity." And, Yeats adds, referring to expectations for his own mind, "To liberate it from all that comes of councils and committees, from the world as it is seen from universities or from populous towns." I tell the class of my own attempts to go beyond the modern discursive mind, to open the mind to the mysteries that are unknown to reason.

Down the road at a farmhouse, pieces of broken mirror glass border the front doorway and all the windows. A neighbor woman tells me this glass will keep the "evil eye," Old Nick the devil, from entering the house. In the evening, John Dooley, a farmer farther down the road, comes to visit. I ask him about the marsh that runs along the farmland. He replies, "Have you heard about the fairies?" He then tells me the story about the farmer near the marsh who had brought a log from the marsh and had placed it beside the fireplace where it remained for twenty-one years. One night, a galloping horse came by the house, and the fairy rider shouted,

"Hurrah, Hurrah. Did you see Dermot?" The log rolled out of the house and onto the horse behind the rider, and they galloped back to the marsh. John Dooley says that he does not believe in fairies but that there are others nearby who still do. The next day I walk to the place where the incident had occurred, and I view the remaining foundation of the abandoned farmhouse.

I start the morning fire in the kitchen stove. The coal burns hesitantly as the coal industry's advertisement on the radio sings out, "A house is not a home if you haven't got a real coal fire." From the window, I watch several lapwings, with their black and white plumage and wispy crests, feeding in the pasture north of the house. Three large hares lope over the frosty field and cross the road at the stone gate. Reading Nolan Jacobson's *Understanding Buddhism*, I am reminded that the concrete event, the momentary *now,* and not abstractions, is all that is real. Everything is abstract except what is happening now; the more we think in abstractions, the more we lose the richness of everyday experience. Missing the reality of this world that is occurring at this moment, I would miss everything. The calculating mind, with its ego-centered, grasping self, destroys the world. But even as I write this, I know that I am engaging in abstraction. The fleeting and momentary now is my concrete experience as I tell a story, yet much of what I tell is an abstraction, a removal from the reality of the eternal now.

On a Saturday night, while still alone, I drive the three miles in the rain to Regan's pub. Driving on the left side of the road is still a dangerous experience. By 9:30, Regan's is filled with local residents sitting around the edges of the dance floor. A Country and Western band, consisting of two guitars, a set of drums, and a piano, begins to play "Tonight I Started Loving You Again." Suddenly I have the feeling that I am in home country. The band plays on, giving a sentimental rendition of "My Bonnie Lies Over the Ocean." The floor is packed with dancers during "Blue Moon of Kentucky." At 11:00, everyone stands for the singing in Gaelic of the Irish national anthem. I drive home to the house that gradually is becoming familiar.

A book that I have brought with me to Ireland is *Samadhi*, by Mike Sayama, on the interpenetration of the self with all things. At the right moment now, I am informed by the author: "The task before us is no longer to differentiate from nature and develop the ego, but transcend the ego and realize the true Self that is one with the universe." Only then can one be at home. Lin-Chi, a ninth-century Chinese Zen master, said, "Make yourself master everywhere, and wherever you stand is the true place." To know peace and harmony means to be in accord with all that is beyond the self, all that is universal and eternal. I know that the sense of feeling at home, of peace and harmony, will come only with an awareness of the oneness of all things and the transcendence of this small self to the wholeness of the universe.

By the next Saturday night, Valerie and Anne have arrived, and we sit around the kitchen table while Anne reads my fortune in the Tarot cards. I ask, "What is the nature of my work?" Selecting the Magic Seven Spread, Anne lays out the cards: the Pope, the Moon, Three of Coins, the Magician, Eight of Cudgels, Lightning, and King of Coins. I learn that I am indeed in a dark time. But in the near future, I will come into a new phase. It will be enhanced by a magical place (Ireland?). There will be contentment. The last card, the King of Coins, has the character of Gemini: "He should budget his energies so that a scattering of his forces will not dissipate his true talents." Gemini, I am told, is not bound by material motives. I am advised by the cards: "Instead of changing occupations, he should use his mental agility to discover new methods in the one he has chosen." The envi-

ronment of Gemini is where the wind blows and the land is rolling and covered with grass.

For a week, I lie aching in bed with Asian flu. When awake, I read *The Diamond Sutra*. The Sutra was translated into Chinese from a Sanskrit text in the fifth century and into English only in recent times. It stresses that transcendence of the conditioned consciousness cannot be accomplished by purely intellectual means or by categories derived from rational modes of thought. The higher wisdom can be attained only with the loss of the conditioned ego and the realization of the transcendental Self. This requires not only regular meditation but also an attitude of relaxed impersonality in all activities and relationships, without attachment to appearances.

In a related text, the *Lankavatara Sutra*, the Buddha is reported to have said, "It is not the mind that is assured, but the heart. The Bodhisattva's assurance arises with the intuition released through removal of the hindrances of passion, dissolution of hindrances of knowledge, and the awakening of egolessness." All conditioned things arise from the discursive thought of the ego-centered self. When this is understood, in concentration and meditation, both discursiveness and the greed of the attached personality cease. By the end of the week, I know intellectually what is to be done. Yet, as always in this journey to a far place, to the place that is right here now, realization comes from a source removed from the conditioned mind.

I remain weak from the flu for several weeks. Throughout this time, I miss my home and friends in DeKalb. Driving to Galway to lecture on modern thought, I take the long way out to the main road. In a book of Irish proverbs, I have read, "The longest road out is the shortest road home." This week, the *Irish Times* begins a series of articles on the plight of the many people who are emigrating from Ireland. On the car radio an Irish country singer ends his song, "Walking on the sidewalks of Chicago—wishing I'd lived another time." Later in the week, we attend the Druid Theater's production of *Bailegangaire*, a new play by the Irish playwright Tom Murphy. The play is about coming home, coming back to the place where ancestors and family have shared laughter and tragedy together for a long time.

As the sun rises earlier each morning, blackbirds call from the shaggy elms in front of the house. This season, all things are happening without conscious effort. Actually, I am giving attention to the inner work of spiritual awareness and, at the same time, I am giving less attention to accumulating knowledge. Once again I am inspired by Lao Tzu:

If we learn, we gain knowledge day by day.
If we act according to the Way, we lose day by day.
We keep losing until we no longer possess anything
  to do.
In non-action we do everything.

This ancient Chinese philosophy continues today in Zen. The modern-day Zen master Tanouye writes: "If you walk one step at a time without thinking anything, just one step at a time, like crawling up a mountain, eventually you will get there." When the top of the mountain is reached, the top is the bottom, and it only took one step to reach the top.

In my journal, I note, sometime while being discursive and mindful, that as we mature we move beyond the rational and linear mode of thought to a more intuitive and transcendent mode. As we make the shift, we begin to lose the grasping and craving self of the individualized ego and find ourselves in the realm of the universal Self. Thus it is not natural for the academic, the intellectual (scientist, sociologist) to continue in the purely rational mode of speculative and dualistic thought as he or she matures and grows older, although this is the approved form for the modern intellectual. To continue solely in the modern rational mode of thought

is retrogressive for the maturing person. Yet we are expected to continue in a thought form that is appropriate only for the middle stages of life.

I have come to the realization, at this point of my life, near to my Celtic ancestors and to Saint Brendan, that reasoned thought alone cannot answer the important existential questions of being human, of being human in relation to the whole world. And I am aware that the cultivation of the vital energy of the universe, rather than intellectual speculation, is the way to self-realization and a compassionate way of being in the world. The way is simple, too simple for the rational mind to comprehend readily.

The wholeness of the universe is sensed in the practice of meditation and the meditative living of each day. Sayama, the author of *Samadhi*, observes, "Breathing in rhythm with the pulsation of the universe is the basic practice of the Way." When a person becomes one with the universe, in the absolute present, that person is then effective in the everyday world. But, Sayama writes, "When one clings to rationality and the ego as the final realities, one is trapped in the phenomenal world of memories taking form according to his attachments and cannot transcend the suffering inherent in dualism." Once we have mastered rationality and moved to the possibilities of intuition and wisdom, we can begin to live in compassionate oneness with all that is.

I have come to know the truth of Sayama's conclusion: "At the most mature level of human being, a person realizes the true self, which is one with the universe and experiences a meaning beyond question and articulation. Such a person transcends anxiety, is fearless, and is moved by compassion." The mature, advanced stage of thought and being goes beyond discursive knowledge and purely rational inquiry. Rather than a life primarily of scholarly production and acquisition, life now demands an inner awakening, a life lived as a work of spiritual enlightenment. The teacher of Saint Theresa advised, "The soul enjoys silence and peace, not by many reasonings, but by simply contemplating the Truth."

My reading has become more an occasion for meditative reflection than an accumulation of knowledge. Whatever the subject, my mind neither craves the discriminating analysis nor finds meaning in such analysis. I read only a few books, especially those that contain the sacred texts of religious traditions and the esoteric writings of spiritual perception. I read again, in this Celtic landscape, *The Upanishads* and *The Bhagavad Gita*, the wisdom literature of early Hinduism.

The message of these writings is that the truth of the universe can be known only through union with Brahman, not through mere learning. The spirit of Brahman is manifest within each of us as that which is called Atman. The translator of *The Upanishads* observes, "God must not be sought as something far away, separate from us, but rather as the very inmost of us, the higher Self in us above the limitations of our little self." In Christian terms, Saint John of the Cross wrote, "In order to find the joy of All, do not desire to enjoy anything." Brahman, who is god, the mystery and truth of the universe, is immanent and transcendent in everything, within each of us, and outside everything. Wherever we are, Brahman can be experienced; we do not have to go anyplace else. In contemplation and meditation the eternal can be seen in all things that pass away. This is the message of the sacred writings, and all spiritual efforts and our artistic and scientific productions are only a variation on this message.

I am trying to know the spiritual center that places me in oneness with all. "Seek ye first the kingdom of God"; this is the great adventure, a voyage beyond the ego-centered, conditioned self. And all that I now experience, both in the East and in the West, tells me that this inner awakening is to be found beyond the rational thought of the trained intellect. I sense the way as I walk down the road to Annaghdown, passing thatched cottages and watching newborn lambs running in the fields.

This life of giving attention to spiritual matters, of going beyond the self to all that is in the world, is a socially committed life. The contemplative life is not self-indulgent, for social issues cannot be faced appropriately without inner spiritual preparation. Oppression in the world is caused by selves that are not spiritually aware, by those who live by greed, fear, egoism, and the craving for power over others. As Jacob Needleman argues in *Lost Christianity*, the "outer" world is not out there, and the "inner" world is not the world of emotions and thought. Both are of the same space, an interpenetration of everything. And in Buddhism, we learn that there is the possibility of attaining the higher spiritual life and escaping the lower life. The Buddha taught the gaining of enlightenment, not by going into some eternal retreat, but by entering fully into everyday life. The objective of spiritual growth is a compassionate living of each moment with all other beings.

During the night, the western wind still beats against the house. In Saint Brendan's voyage, a favorable wind blew after the boat had been adrift: "God raised a wind favorable to them again, from west to east." Saint Brendan and his crew then "let the boat go wherever the wind would drive it." The wind becomes calm as the sun rises now early in the morning. A song thrush, high on the telephone pole beside the house, repeatedly calls and sings its song. The hawthorn on the banks of the narrow road is beginning to bloom. White mute swans have returned to the lake in the marsh, and the slopes are covered with the golden flowering furze bush. In the evening the call of the cuckoo is heard across the lake.

What the voyage has come to is the realization that no amount of theorizing and rational thinking can tell me much about reality. To enter into the unknown and eternal realm requires a mind that is in a state of detachment and compassion. In a book on the perennial philosophy, Aldous Huxley has written: "It is a fact, confirmed and re-confirmed during two or three thousand years of religious history, that the ultimate Reality is not clearly and immediately apprehended, except by those who have made themselves loving, pure in heart and poor in spirit." Only when we allow the eternal Self to dwell in the depths of the particular self and only when the ego-centered, rational self is lost can the mystery of the universe be apprehended.

And the final expression of this awareness may not be in more talk and more words, but in silence. As Saint John of the Cross observed, "For whereas speaking distracts, silence and work collect thoughts and strengthen the spirit." With the wisdom gained by awareness, there may be no further need to talk and to write discursively. One then practices what is realized with attention and silence, in charity and humility.

*I have come to the realization,
at this point in my life, near to my Celtic ancestors and to Saint
Brendan, that reasoned thought alone cannot answer the important
existential questions of being human, of being human in relation to the
whole world. And I am aware that the cultivation of the vital energy of
the universe rather than intellectual speculation, is the way to self-
realization and a compassionate way of
being in the world.*

St. Brendan's Monastery, Annaghdown, Ireland, winter 1986

To keep Old Nick away

Thatched farmhouse, Corrandulla, Ireland

The coming of spring

On the Headford Road

· *On the Way Home* ·

THE STRUGGLE FOR PEACE in this life continues each day. The dark voyage beyond the self to a home that is everywhere in the world has led to a spiritual crisis, to what may be renewal if the path can be walked gracefully.

Reader and fellow traveler, I had hoped to conclude with a sense of fulfillment that might console the hearts and minds of those who have chosen to wander this world on the journey toward home. But we continue on the journey, and home is not to be found in any conclusion. The journey is the only home we have. As we travel, we are on the way home.

Perhaps in another telling of this journey, I can find a form appropriate to the emerging spiritual being. At this point, it is a fleeting and scattered self, one with several voices and identities on the path toward home. Any writing is a representation of this changing self that seeks union with the larger Self of all creation. The voices speak, and the mind watches and listens and says, "Let go, let go."

•

The journey inward is a journey beyond the barrier of the self. The one who travels inward becomes infinite in time and space. This teaching is expressed clearly in the Sanskrit formula *tat tvam asi:* "Thou art that." The traveler is thus on the way toward oneness with Atman, with the eternal Self. The traveler's quest is to discover the fact of *tat tvam asi,* to find the immanent meaning of existence. The absolute principle of existence is within each of us. And the farther we travel inward, the farther we travel outward. The inward journey is to a far place, one that is the whole of existence. The truth can be grasped only when we are no longer ourselves, when we are beyond the constructions of the grasping self. Only when we are "nothing," in Zen terms, are we then enlightened.

In a recent spiritual reading, you were told that in a former life you were a religious being, perhaps a cleric or a monk. The place might have been China, or maybe Ireland. "I can't be certain," she said. Certainly you realized at an early time that all life is transient, that nothing that exists is permanent. You have confronted the self before and have walked in the raging storm of the dark night. Your work has been hard, and you have worked to free the mind in order to feel the loving-kindness that embraces all things.

Yes, I have come to realize that nothing in the world has any essential value. There is nothing solid and unchanging that can

154

be called a self. The forest monk of Thailand, Achaan Chah, says, "Ultimately no one exists, only earth, fire, water, and air—elements that have combined temporarily. We call the body a person, my self, but ultimately there is no me, there is only *anata,* not-self." Once not-self is understood in the heart, everything is lighter and everyday life is filled with compassion.

Perhaps this awareness of impermanence, suffering, and emptiness is a cause of your current spiritual crisis. Practice daily this awareness. If you know that there is no *why* to be answered by the restless mind, then there can be peace. Learn to be still. In stillness comes the true joy of the Buddha.

I will watch the river flow. I will walk the forest path in stillness and in compassion. I will live each day in the light of the universe. I will not try to be anything.

Home is no longer a dwelling place, but it is life being lived. The journey is a healing of the separation from the eternal. Our modern homelessness is transcended in an awareness of our oneness with all other beings, in an awareness of our oneness with the divine mystery of the universe. We struggle personally and collectively in this world to find our true home.

•

During my final weeks in Ireland, I felt more than ever the tension between my practice and the demands of everyday life. Even with the knowledge of impermanence, I was still pulled by, attached to, the modern struggle for meaning. My practice had become isolated and unfocused in this foreign place. At the same time, I had lost the passion for the achievement of the worldly things that had once engaged me. Another research project, another book, another worldly experience would not help in this crisis

of the spirit. Any future work would have to be a reflection of my search for a spiritual home.

I listened on the radio to Samuel Beckett's words about the nature of human life: We are born, we live, we die, and we cannot remain silent. We cannot remain silent, and yet I knew the truth of silence. Reading *Zen Flesh, Zen Bones*, I found the ancient Chinese commentary:

Words cannot describe everything.
The heart's message cannot be delivered in words.
If one receives words literally, he will be lost.
If he tries to explain with words, he will not attain enlightenment in this life.

Within the void, the emptiness of all, it is silence that holds us together.

It had come to the matter of right understanding. And right understanding could be found only in further practice. I discovered the advice of Shunryu Suzuki: "When you can sit with your whole body and mind, and with the oneness of your mind and body under the control of the universal mind, you can easily attain this kind of right understanding. Your everyday life will be renewed without being attached to an old erroneous interpretation of life." As I read this and understood it clearly, I knew that my suffering would not be ended by further contemplation of philosophy. Only through practice in everyday life could this suffering be ended.

Is it not true, that after all these years, it is the heart that is asking to be heard?

The heart, yes, and all the attention that one gives to the loving of others.

How did you feel, then, when you took her to the early morning train in Galway, the train that would take her far away?

It seemed to be an ending of sorts. I would have to live without knowing, trying

*The absolute principle of existence
is within each of us. And the farther we travel inward, the farther we
travel outward. The inward journey is to a far place, one that is
the whole of existence.*

Prairie winter, DeKalb County (this page and following four pages)

to accept the truth that everything changes. As I walked along the Annaghdown road, the bachelor farmer greeted me with a hardy, "Morning." I answered, "Morning." "Fine," he said. "It is," I replied.

You would then be open to your suffering? Be aware of all suffering from warfare to poverty to the suffering of the self. Keep your heart open to the suffering "out there" and the suffering within. Know the suffering that is created in the mind—sadness, depression, and fear. Turn your suffering into awareness and compassion.

I will practice the Sanskrit teaching: "At the start of sneezing, during fright, in anxiety, above a chasm, flying in battle, in extreme curiosity, at the beginning of hunger, at the end of hunger, be uninterruptedly *aware*." When we are in difficulty or distress, we have the possibility of enlightenment.

Then consider this: Could it be that your practice has activated a spiritual energy that has brought about what transpersonal psychologists call a "spiritual emergency"? The crisis has the potential of allowing you to rise to a higher state of being. A spiritual emergency might result in spiritual healing and a renewal.

I cannot accept everyday life as before, or be satisfied with it. There is a homesickness of the spirit, a longing for a life beyond the ordinary consciousness of gaining and spending. I would be happy to leave no trace beyond the compassionate living of each moment. Within this crisis, I sense the joy of moving toward a divine fulfillment. As this self of small proportion is gradually lost, I begin to commune with the universal life.

Spiritual growth does not express itself gently. Do your spiritual work; practice each moment of your life. Help all others in their suffering.

•

We are seekers, travelers on the way who desire to reach the other shore. By opening ourselves, we make ourselves ready for the journey. In Christian terms (Matthew 5:6), we read: "Blessed are they which do hunger and thirst after righteousness: for they shall be filled." The journey toward righteousness is within, and it is undertaken not for the result itself, not to solve sorrow and suffering, but for its own spiritual sake.

The paradox of the Zen way is that the harder we seek, the less likely we are to be enlightened, to be saved. Like chasing our shadow, the harder we run to catch it, the faster it moves away. Suzuki writes in *Zen Mind, Beginner's Mind*: "When you try to attain enlightenment, then you have a big burden on your mind. Your mind will not be clear enough to see things as they are. If you truly see things as they are, then you will see things as they should be." Only by not being attached to the journey, by being mindful, do we find what we need.

Yet, and this is the other side of the paradox, if we do not seek, if we do not try to be mindful, we will not attain spiritual fulfillment. One must work at the spiritual life in order for it to be revealed. The heart is open to spiritual growth when the mind is watchful. Seeking is simply the practice of being mindful. Suzuki concludes: "Wherever you go you should be the master of your surroundings. This means you should not lose your way." Always be on the path, on the journey toward home.

One task I had remaining in Ireland was to find the birthplace of my great-grandparents, John and Bridget. It was a search for the remains of a physical identity, for the origins of this self that is being lost to something greater. Traveling to Kilkenny and walking along an overgrown boreen and into a woods, I found the one-acre field that had been home to my ancestors. Anne and I photographed the remains and made our way out to the main road.

And now, you are satisfied in some way that you have found your home?

Home is back on the road, on the journey beyond place and time. Home is mindfully living in the present, living the life unencumbered by the past and by expectation of the future. There is joy in being mindful along the way.

You travel a path, then, rather than being guided by a system of speculations and explanations?

Yes, but there is still a pursuit of the truth, a desire to go to the root of things. And this is beyond human constructions of reality.

It is an inquiry into the mystery of all being, beyond words, through the heart.

I will speak only what is useful and necessary. It is finally a matter of virtue: taking care that I do not harm others by thought, word, or deed. I like the insight of Achaan Chah: "Only when our words and deeds come from kindness can we quiet the mind and open the heart." Learning to watch the breath, watching the mind and actions in everyday life, I may grow in wisdom and compassion.

This is the way of a very simple journey.

•

A home for the self is found only when the self becomes a part of everything else. The ego-self is lost as it becomes one with the universe. This is how one finally finds a home, a journey inward to the whole of existence. This is the home place.

What is left for the inquiring mind, then, if the true reality is beyond the self and its thoughts? If all conceptual knowledge of the ego-self is relative, what is the place of thought and its interpretation of lived experience? In this age, how is the perceptual world held together? How is one to have right perception?

Our human constructions, our concepts of reality, are the shadows of existence. The shadows are not the reality, but are merely the conditioned speculations. As soon as the human mind begins to construct a reality, it loses the essence of the ultimate and true reality.

It is with such awareness that all esoteric traditions emphasize a quieting of the mind in order to perceive the world. Knowledge is gained through clear perception, when the knower and the known have become one, rather than by "rational" speculation or the gathering of "empirical" evidence. The critical mind in the esoteric tradition is a mind that is open, therefore quiet and calm, and a mind that neither accepts or rejects, but one that goes beyond judgments, beyond conditioned knowledge. Right perception, including the moral action that follows, comes out of the silent mind, the mind that is now heart as well as mind. We begin to see clearly when we are on the way home.

Suchness is the Zen term for the quality of the experience before thought and interpretation. Before comment, before judgment, things are just as they are. This is the emptiness of all phenomena in their actuality. The complexity of thought removes us from this true reality. Insight takes us into the reality of all things. As we unlearn the busy patterns of thought, we begin to see clearly and to understand.

The truth is unknown to the learned mind, as taught in *The Upanishads*. Truth is known to the clear mind, to the pure heart. Truth is not found in philosophical argumentation. The scriptures (Matthew 6:33) proclaim: "Seek ye first the Kingdom of God, and his righteousness." All other things will be added.

Yet the spiritual life is a work of creation. Everyone is given the inner light of the spirit. Miseries of the world are caused by the lack of insight. Accept the wisdom of insight as a divine gift, seeing clearly all things as they are. Insight is not complex, speculative, or analytical. It is the inner light of the heart.

I would continue to practice what I was learning each day on the journey. I would watch in a very simple way. Insight, rather than accumulated knowledge and complex analysis, would be the source of understanding. The eloquence of simplicity, free of the conditioned mind, would be observed. Inward and outward, more of my life would be in silence.

•

On the way home:

Try to be mindful, and let things take their natural course. Then your mind will become still in any surroundings, like a clear forest pool. All kinds of wonderful, rare animals will come to drink at the pool, and you will clearly see the nature of all things. You will see many strange and wonderful things come and go, but you will be still. This is the happiness of the Buddha.

This much Achaan Chah taught. "You will reach a point where the heart tells itself what to do."

The forest path is one that wanders. The way is known only in the traveling. The patient traveler follows the path wherever it leads. There may be few signs along the way. And the end is never in sight.

The journey home is no more or less than the enlightenment that comes with the living of each moment, day by day, step by step. The way is simple, yet the truth must constantly be repeated: Thou art that. I am the whole of reality, the mystery of the universe. Home is just that much.

On the farm, near the marsh

BIBLIOGRAPHY

Aitken, Robert. *The Mind of Clover: Essays in Zen Buddhist Ethics*. San Francisco: North Point Press, 1984.

Bachelard, Gaston. *The Poetics of Space*. Translated by Maria Jolas. Boston: Beacon Press, 1969.

Barthes, Roland. *Camera Lucida: Reflections on Photography*. Translated by Richard Howard. New York: Hill and Wang, 1981.

Bashō, Matsuo. *The Narrow Road to the Deep North and Other Travel Sketches*. Translated by Nobuyuki Yuasa. New York: Penguin, 1966.

Batchelor, Stephen. *Alone with Others: An Existential Approach to Buddhism*. New York: Grove Press, 1983.

Bhagavad Gita, The. Translated by Juan Mascaró. New York: Penguin, 1962.

Blanchot, Maurice. *The Space of Literature*. Translated by Ann Smock. Lincoln: University of Nebraska Press, 1982.

Bly, Robert. *The Kabir Book: Forty-four of the Ecstatic Poems of Kabir*. Boston: Beacon Press, 1977.

Bukkyo Dendo Kyokai. *The Teaching of Buddha*. Tokyo: Buddhist Promoting Foundation, 1966.

Campbell, Joseph. *The Hero with a Thousand Faces*. 2nd ed. Princeton: Princeton University Press, 1968.

Camus, Albert. *The Myth of Sisyphus*. Translated by Justin O'Brien. New York: Knopf, 1955.

Cavell, Stanley. *The Senses of Walden*. San Francisco: North Point Press, 1981.

Chah, Achaan. *A Still Forest Pool*. Edited by Jack Kornfield and Paul Breiter. Wheaton, Ill.: Theosophical Publishing House, 1985.

Ch'en, Kenneth K. S. *The Chinese Transformation of Buddhism*. Princeton: Princeton University Press, 1973.

Clayre, Alasdair. *The Heart of the Dragon*. Boston: Houghton Mifflin, 1984.

Dhammapada, The. Translated by Irving Babbitt. New York: New Directions, 1936.

Dhammapada, The. Translated by Juan Mascaró. New York: Penguin, 1973.

Diamond Sutra, The, with supplemental texts. Edited by Raghavan Iyer. Santa Barbara: Concord Grove Press, 1983.

Dürckheim, Karlfried. *The Way of Transformation: Daily Life as Spiritual Exercise*. London: George Allen and Unwin, 1971.

Eiseley, Loren. "The Chesmologue." In *The Night Country*. New York: Scribner's, 1971.

————. *The Innocent Assassins*. New York: Scribner's, 1973.

Eliade, Mircea. *The Sacred and the Profane: The Nature of Religion*. Translated by Willard R. Trask. New York: Harcourt, Brace and World, 1959.

Emerson, Ralph Waldo. "The American Scholar." In *Selected Writings of Ralph Waldo Emerson*, edited by William H. Gilman. New York: New American Library, 1965.

Flanagan, John T. "The Reality of Midwestern Literature." In Thomas T. McAvoy et al., *The Midwest: Myth or Reality*. Notre Dame: University of Notre Dame Press, 1961.

Grof, Christina, and Stanislav Grof. "Spiritual Emergency: The Understanding and Treatment of Transpersonal Crises," *ReVision* 8 (Winter/Spring 1986): 7–20.

Hanh, Thich Nhat. *The Miracle of Mindfulness: A*

Manual on Meditation. Boston: Beacon Press, 1976.

Hesse, Herman. *Siddhartha*. Translated by Hilda Rosner. New York: New Directions, 1951.

Huxley, Aldous. *The Perennial Philosophy*. New York: Harper & Row, 1970 (1945).

Jackson, J. B. *The Necessity for Ruins, and Other Topics*. Amherst: University of Massachusetts Press, 1980.

Jacobson, Nolan Pliny. *Understanding Buddhism*. Carbondale: Southern Illinois University Press, 1986.

Kierkegaard, Søren. *The Sickness unto Death*. Edited and translated by Howard V. Hong and Edna H Hong. Princeton: Princeton University Press, 1980.

Krishnamurti, J. *The Flight of the Eagle*. New York: Harper & Row, 1971.

———. *You Are the World*. New York: Harper & Row, 1972.

———. *The Wholeness of Life*. New York: Harper & Row, 1979.

———. *Freedom from the Known*. New York: Harper & Row, 1975.

———. *Krishnamurti's Notebook*. New York: Harper & Row, 1976.

Lagerkvist, Pär. *Evening Land*. Translated by W. H. Auden and Leif Sjobert. Detroit: Wayne State University Press, 1975.

Lao Tzu. *The Way of Lao Tzu*. Translated by Wing-Tsit Chan. Indianapolis: Bobbs-Merrill, 1963.

———. *Tao Te Ching*. Translated by Gia-Fu Feng and Jane English. New York: Random House, 1972.

Le Guin, Ursula K. "It Was a Dark and Stormy Night: or, Why Are We Huddling about the Campfire?" *Critical Inquiry* 7 (Autumn 1980): 191–199.

Lovecraft, H. P. *The Case of Charles Dexter Ward*. New York: Ballantine, 1971 (1941).

McLuhan, T. C. *Touch the Earth: A Self-Portrait of Indian Existence*. New York: Simon and Schuster, 1971.

Maezumi, Hakuyu Taizan. *The Way of Everyday Life*. Los Angeles: Zen Center, 1978.

Masters, Edgar Lee. "George Gray." In *Spoon River Anthology*. New York: Macmillan, 1962.

Meing, D. W., ed. *The Interpretation of Ordinary Landscapes: Geographical Essays*. New York: Oxford University Press, 1979.

Merton, Thomas. *The Wisdom of the Desert*. New York: New Directions, 1960.

———. *The Way of Chuang Tzu*. New York: New Directions, 1965.

———. *The Silent Life*. New York: Farrar, Straus and Giroux. New York: Noonday, 1975.

Monod, Jacques. *Chance and Necessity*. New York: Vintage, 1972.

Needleman, Jacob. *Lost Christianity*. New York: Harper & Row, 1980.

Nishitani, Keiji. *Religion and Nothingness*. Translated by Jan Van Bragt. Berkeley: University of California Press, 1982.

O'Faolain, Sean. *The Irish*. Harmondsworth, England: Penguin, 1947.

Prigogine, Ilya, and Isabelle Stengers. *Order Out of Chaos: Man's New Dialogue with Nature*. New York: Bantam, 1984.

Quinney, Richard. *The Social Reality of Crime*. Boston: Little, Brown, 1970.

———. "From Repression to Liberation: Social Theory in a Radical Age." In *Theoretical Perspectives on Deviance*, edited by Robert A. Scott and Jack D. Douglas. New York: Basic Books, 1972.

———. *Providence: The Reconstruction of Social and Moral Order*. New York: Longman, 1980.

———. *Social Existence: Metaphysics, Marxism, and the Social Sciences*. Beverly Hills: Sage, 1982.

Ravindra, Ravi. *Whispers from the Other Shore: A Spiritual Search—East and West*. Wheaton, Ill.: Theosophical Publishing House, 1984.

Reps, Paul. Comp. *Zen Flesh, Zen Bones*. New York: Penguin, 1971.

Rilke, Rainer Maria. *Selected Poems of Rainer Maria Rilke*. Translated by Robert Bly New York: Harper & Row, 1981.

Sayama, Mike. *Samadhi: Self Development in Zen, Swordsmanship, and Psychotherapy*. Albany: State University of New York Press, 1986.

Seung Sahn. *Only Don't Know*. San Francisco: Four Seasons, 1982.

Stryk, Lucien. *Encounter with Zen*. Athens: Ohio University Press, 1981.

Suzuki, Shunryu. *Zen Mind, Beginner's Mind*. New York: Weatherhill, 1970.

Thoreau, Henry D. *Walden*. Edited by J. Lyndon Shaley. Princeton: Princeton University Press, 1973.

Tillich, Paul. *The Shaking of the Foundations*. New York: Scribner's, 1965.

Tuan, Yi-Fu. *Space and Place: The Perspective of Experience*. Minneapolis: University of Minnesota Press, 1977.

Upanishads, The. Translated by Juan Mascaró. New York: Penguin, 1965.

Voyage of Saint Brendan, The. Translated by John J. O'Meara, Mountrath, Ireland: Dolmen Press, 1978.

Watts, Alan W. *The Way of Zen*. New York: Random House, 1957.

Weyl, Herman. *Philosophy of Mathematics and Natural Science*. Princeton: Princeton University Press, 1949.

Wittgenstein, Ludwig. *Tractatus Logico-Philosophicus*. Translated by C. K. Ogden. London: Routledge and Kegan Paul, 1981.

Wordsworth, William. "The Ruined Cottage." In *The Poems of William Wordsworth*, edited by Jonathan Wordsworth. Cambridge, England: University Printing House, 1973.

Wright, Charles. "Lonesome Pine Special." In *The Other Side of the River*. New York: Vintage, 1984.

Yeats, William Butler. *Mythologies*. New York: Collier, 1959.

Zimmerman, Michael E. *Eclipse of the Self: The Development of Heidegger's Concept of Authenticity*. Athens: Ohio University Press, 1982.